Generation to Generation

Stanley Papel

Luminare Press
www.luminarepress.com

Front Cover Images

Top photos - Left to right

1. Isaac Goldman (Great Grandfather to Stanley Papel) along with his 4th or 5th wife,
2. Mike and Effie Roth (Grandparents to Stanley Papel)
3. Joseph and Fannie Popelsky (Grandparents to Stanley Papel)
4. Phil and Sophie Papel (Parents to Stanley Papel)

Bottom photos - Left to Right

1. Stanley, Sophie, Phil and Arlene (sister to Stanley Papel) Papel
2. Evan, Phinley, Debbi, Joe and Stanley Papel (son, daughter-in-law and grandchildren to Stanley Papel)

Back Cover Images

Top photos - Left to right

1. Sitting- Ethyl Papel, Mary Socher-Papel, Barry Socher, Rochelle Papel, Arlene Papel, Geraldine Papel, Stanley Papel
2. Standing- Al Socher, Bernie Papel, Sonya Papel, Sol Papel, Jerry Papel, Joseph Popelsky, Fannie Popelsky, Mark Papel, Sophie Papel, Phil Papel

Bottom photos- Left to Right

1. Louis Fisch (Great Grandfather to Stanley Papel)
2. Sophie Fisch (Great Grandmother to Stanley Papel)
3. Abraham Fisch (Great Great Grandfather to Stanley Papel)
4. 4th wife pictured with Josef Roth (Great Grandfather to Stanley Papel)

DISCLAIMER:

This book is memoir. It reflects the author's present recollections of experiences and perceptions over time. It also reflects the recollections of several contributors including those of Phil Papel and Sophie Papel. The manuscript was not intended to hurt anyone. The author does not assume and hereby disclaims any liability to any party for any loss, damage, or disruption caused by errors or omissions, whether such errors or omissions result from negligence, accident, or any other cause. I regret any unintentional discomfort caused by the publication.

Generation to Generation

Copyright © 2020 by Stanley Papel

All rights reserved. This book or any portion thereof may not be reproduced or used in any manner whatsoever without the express written permission of the publisher, except for the use of brief quotations in a book review.

The GENERATION TO GENERATION trademark was assigned a Serial Number #90158826 by the United States Patent and Trademark Office (USPTO).

Printed in the United States of America

Cover and interior layout by Claire Flint Last

Luminare Press
442 Charnelton St.
Eugene, OR 97401
www.luminarepress.com

www.GenerationToGeneration.online
www.stanleypapel.com

LCCN: 2020917374
ISBN: 978-1-64388-429-5

I proudly dedicate this book to my mother, Sophie Papel,
and to the memory of my father, Phil Papel.

Both parents gave me the gift of life and unconditional
love throughout their lives.

I also dedicate this book to the future generations of the Papel family,
who I hope will find our family history to be meaningful.

I never knew any of my great grandparents,
but they made life in America to be something
that I am proud of and thankful for.

Author Gary Seigel on *Generation to Generation*:

"Always fascinating and consistently entertaining, Stan Papel's wonderful autography has a laid-back charm and candid sense of humor that fuels a massive amount of memories, including those of his mother, father, and other members of his family. We get detailed insight into what it was like to grow up in Los Angeles in the 1940s and 1950s. Particularly fascinating is Papel's description of his dad's growth as an entrepreneur from early pioneer in the giftware business and his success in opening one of the first retail gift stores on Disneyland's Main Street to the multi-million dollar expansion that Stan helped create and develop. Though this book may have been written mainly for family and friends, it offers other readers a fascinating and endearing glimpse at the numerous challenges of juggling business, family, children, wife—eventually ex-wife. His insights include an unusually honest assessment of what it was like to struggle with sexual identity, describing in some detail his coming out experience when he was in his 50s. I highly recommend this book."

Gary Seigel is the author of *Haskell Himself,* a new novel from Acorn Press. His nonfiction book, *The Mouth Trap: Strategies, Tips, and Secrets for Keeping Your Feet Out of Your Mouth,* published in 2008 by Career Press, has been translated into a dozen languages.

Corporate/business writer Mark Gauthier on *Generation to Generation*:

"Touching, truly interesting, and well written. Your love of your family is palpable, your challenges around "coming out" honest and not sugar-coated, and your commitment to business success as an engine that drove you both admirable and moving, though you're candid about the cost of success to other areas of your life and well-being. Not to mention that your life story is a virtual 'primer' on the giftware business."

Mark Gauthier is the president of The Foundation for The Palm Springs Unified School District. After a long career as a Madison Avenue advertising and promotion copywriter, with positions on the editorial, advertising, and business sides of *Foreign Affairs, Forbes,* and *TIME* magazines (1980s), he began working independently in New York as a corporate and marketing writer in publishing, media, pharmaceuticals, technology, packaged-goods, automotive, B2B, education, upscale real estate, and other categories.

Table of Contents

Preface ix

PART I: Stanley Papel (1942–) xi

CHAPTER 1
Stanley Papel: Early Memories (1942–1947) 1

CHAPTER 2
Stanley Papel: Family and Friends (1947–1952) 5

CHAPTER 3
Stanley Papel: School Years (1952–1967) 10

CHAPTER 4
Stanley Papel: Bachelor Days (1967–1972) 21

CHAPTER 5
Stanley Papel: Just Married (1972–1978) 25

CHAPTER 6
Stanley Papel: The Up and Down Years (1978–1990) 30

CHAPTER 7
Stanley Papel: Changes are Coming (1990–1995) 35

CHAPTER 8
Stanley Papel: Coming Out Story (1995) 38

CHAPTER 9
Stanley Papel: The Transition Years (1995–1998) 44

CHAPTER 10
Stanley Papel: The Lost Decade (1999–2009) 50

CHAPTER 11
Stanley Papel: The Career Years (1970–2014) 56

CHAPTER 12
Stanley Papel: Travel (1945–2019) 65

CHAPTER 13
Stanley Papel: From Bittersweet to The Golden Years (2016–2019) ... 73

CHAPTER 14
Stanley Papel: Stranger than Life 82

CHAPTER 15
Stanley Papel: Reflections 84

Major Events in the Life of Stanley Papel 86

PART II: Phil Papel (1916–1998) 89
Life Story of Phil Papel by Phil Papel 91

PART III: Sophie Roth Papel (1918–) 117

INTRODUCTION
Sophie Roth Papel (1918–) 119

CHAPTER 1
Sophie Roth Papel: Birth and Babyhood (b. 1918) 120

CHAPTER 2
Sophie Roth Papel: Beginning School (1918–) 122

CHAPTER 3
Sophie Roth Papel: Terrors (1918–) 123

CHAPTER 4
Sophie Roth Papel: Joyous Memories (1918–) 124

CHAPTER 5
Sophie Roth Papel: Vacations (1918–) 126

CHAPTER 6
Sophie Roth Papel: Beyond the School Years (1918–) 129

PART IV: Joseph Popelsky (1876–1964) 135
Joseph Popelsky: (1876–1964) 137

PART V: Fannie Goldman Popelsky (1887–1982) 143
Fannie Goldman Popelsky: (1887–1982) 145

PART VI: Mihaly ("Mike") Roth (1876–1948) 153

CHAPTER 1
Mihaly "Mike" Roth: Childhood Memories (1876–1948) 155

CHAPTER 2
Mihaly "Mike" Roth: School Days (1876–1948) 157

CHAPTER 3
Mihaly "Mike" Roth: Troublesome Days (1876–1948) 159

CHAPTER 4
Mihaly "Mike" Roth: In Budapest (1876–1948) 160

CHAPTER 5
Mihaly "Mike" Roth: In America (1876–1948) 161

PART VII: Effie Fisch Roth (1884–1977) 165
Effie Fisch Roth: (1884–1977) 167

"What's in a Name?" 181
Index of Names 182
Acknowledgments 185
About the Author 186

Louis Fisch

PREFACE

When I was about 10 years old, I asked my Grandma Effie to tell me about her parents—Sophia, whom my mom was named after, and Louis, whom I was named after as Stanley Louis Papel. After telling me many wonderful things about my great grandmother Sophia, all Grandma Effie said about my great grandfather Louis was, "I really don't remember much about him, but I know he was a gambler and a drunk." It always bothered me that she remembered hardly anything about her father and what she did know was very negative.

About 45 years later, in 1996, I was putting up a wall of family photos at my home in West Hollywood, and my eyes locked onto Louis Fisch's photo. As I looked, he seemed to be saying to me, "I was NOT a gambler and a drunk." He had the same eyes as me, and it was as if I saw myself in him. Then I had a troubling thought. "When my great grandchildren ask about me someday, it's possible that my grandchildren might say something like, "I really don't remember much about him, but I know that he divorced his wife because he was gay."

In other words, I would be identified by some things that don't fully recognize me for who I am. Maybe Great Grandfather Louis may have gambled and liked to drink, but there was a lot more to him than those two negative characteristics. It's the same with me and with everyone. We should not reduce people to labels and think that we know them.

For example, cousin Geri Roth Jacobson mentioned that Louis had written many letters to his daughters, which were kept in an old trunk—a trunk that was passed over the years from family to family. When I asked Geri if she could retrieve the letters, she said she had heard that they had been burned. Why that happened is a mystery, but I believe that the letters would have revealed Louis to have been a far more complex person than my grandmother's description: a kind man who loved his daughters. As the years pass, I have looked at his photo several times, and I keep hearing in my mind, "I am a lot more than a gambler and a drunk."

One of the incentives for me to write this book is to show that there is much more to people—including those in our family—than the simplistic labels we apply to them. I don't have any great grandchildren yet, but if they read this book, they will know that there was much more to me than my sexual orientation, which is a small part of who I am.

"Who am I?" is a question we all ask ourselves during our lifetimes. Perhaps by understanding our parents' and grandparents' lives, we might find a partial answer to this question. This book is an attempt to write about my life, and the lives of my parents, their parents and grandparents. Whatever I can obtain of our family history I will try to include, as I know this information will someday be meaningful to future generations of our family.

I don't consider my own life story to be overly exciting. I am somewhat of a private and introverted person; therefore, it will take some courage to be open about some of the thoughts and experiences that I have kept to myself. The other personal stories here may also be uncomfortable to read or very personal, but it's important for these things to be revealed so we can appreciate our family history in its entirety and know who we are.

I think of what is written on my father's gravestone: "As long as we live, he too shall live." Similarly, as long as future generations read and add to this family history, the people in it will continue to live.

PART I
Stanley Papel
(1942–)

ANCESTRY CHART FOR STANLEY PAPEL

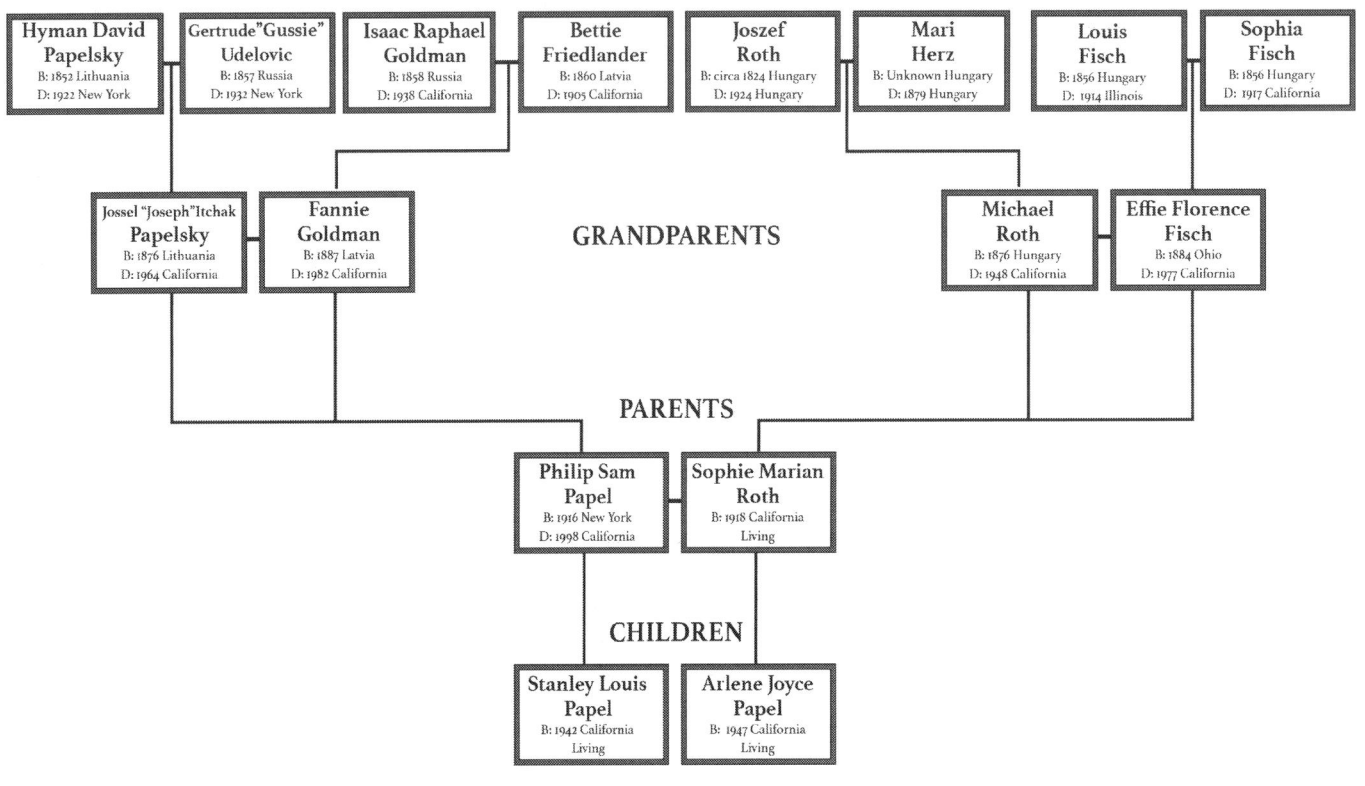

DESCENDENTS OF STANLEY PAPEL & AILEEN MILLER

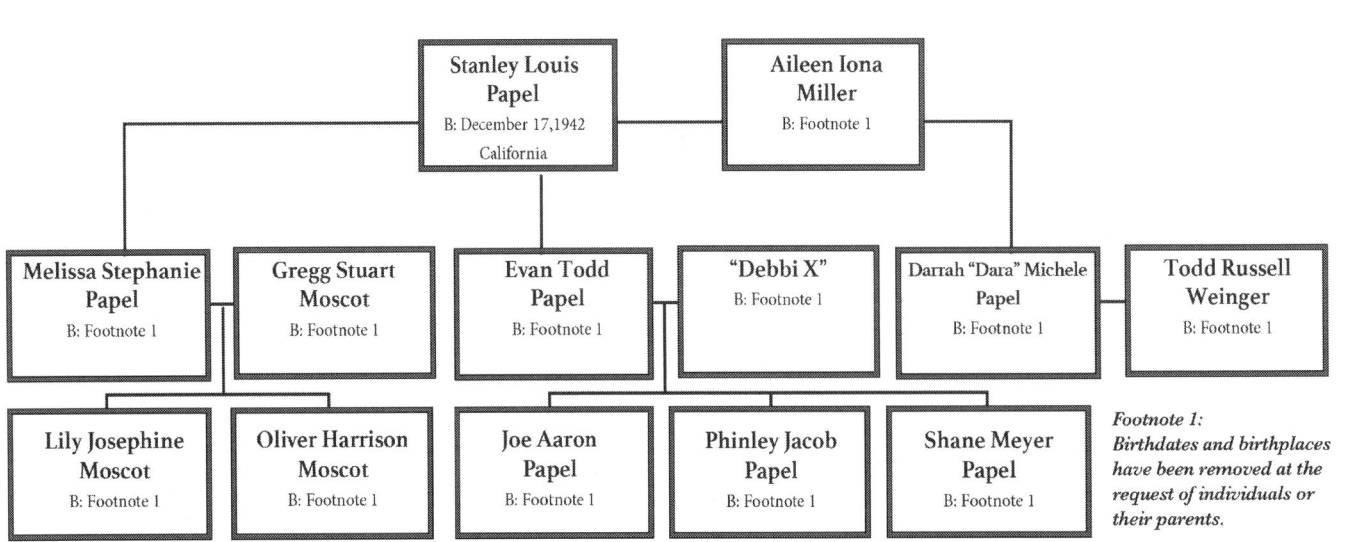

Footnote 1: Birthdates and birthplaces have been removed at the request of individuals or their parents.

CHAPTER 1

Stanley Papel
Early Memories (1942–1947)

On December 16, 1942, at 11:00 p.m., my mother checked into Cedars of Lebanon Hospital in Los Angeles. I finally made my appearance into this world on December 17, 1942, at 4:00 p.m. My parents, Sophie and Phil Papel, told me I put up quite a battle in deciding whether to give up the comfort of the womb. My dad jokingly reminded me that the 11:00 p.m. check-in cost him an extra day at the hospital; twenty-five dollars for a hospital room was a lot of money in those days! I was born during World War II, a difficult time for many people. Accordingly, my parents lived in a small apartment. When I was about 6 months old, my father joined the Navy, and my mother and I moved to my grandparents' home, Mike and Effie Roth's, at 1545 Third Avenue, Los Angeles, California, where I remember living with my mom in the rear bedroom at the same house where she was born and raised. My mom and I lived there until my father was discharged in 1945, when the three of us moved to a duplex a few blocks away on Cochran Avenue, which I remember well.

My earliest memory is when I was about 2-years old. It is a little embarrassing as a first thing in my life to remember. It was during the war. My father had a weekend leave in San Diego while my mother and grandmother went out for the evening, leaving Grandpa Mike to care of me. He put me on the potty and I made a "big success," as my Grandma Effie fondly referred to it. However, when it came to wiping my bottom, my grandpa did not do a very good job. As a matter of fact, if my memory serves me right, he forgot to wipe me. I tried to tell him to wipe my bottom, but I think this was before I could talk clearly. He did not understand me, so I cried and cried. When I saw my mom the next day, I told her in my baby talk what had not happened while my grandpa was babysitting me. All I can say now is that it is an embarrassing early memory. I had three birthdays at my grandparents' home. I remember well my third birthday party—even recalling some of the guests that were invited, who were mostly family members. My family was very close in those days. My mother had two first cousins who were like sisters to her. Stephanie Leff was the daughter of Hattie Blume; and Marian Ullman was the daughter of Fannie Cohen. My grandmother, Effie, was very close with her sisters, Fannie and Hattie. The three sisters all lived together at the same house at 1545 Third Avenue after World War II when my mom and I moved out.

Actually, it is quite amazing how many memories are coming back to me. I recall times before my 4th birthday of my grandfather taking me for walks. He had a cane, and he let me use it during our walks. I remember my grandmother taking me downtown with her on the red streetcars that ran along Venice Boulevard. We would go to the bank, and into the vault, and I would see what looked like thousands of boxes. Grandma Effie told me she kept valuable papers in there. Years later, after she died, I found out that she had been buying U.S. Saving Bonds for all her grandchildren over the years and that they were probably some of the valuables that were kept there. My grandfather also had a few commemorative coins in there which Grandma Effie gave to me when I was a child. I still have those coins, which I would never part with. Other memories pertain to some of the vintage appliances in the Third Avenue house. The telephone was the kind that had the earpiece receiver separate from the mouthpiece, and both were mounted on the wall. I remember that when they got a new phone, a table model, and my grandparents' phone number changed from Prospect 5017 to Republic 45107. That was well before area codes were in existence. My grandparents had an old-fashioned icebox; a bathtub that was probably the original when they moved into the Third Avenue house in 1918; and a chamber pot that they kept in the closet. Of course, I went back to the house many times over the years until my grandmother finally moved a few years before she died, so my memories of the place were periodically reinforced. We used to have our Thanksgiving family get-togethers at that house each year throughout my childhood.

My first memories of my mom are from the house on Third Avenue, but I do not remember my father until we were getting ready to move from that home into the duplex nearby on Cochran Ave. I was closer with my mother than my father because he was in the service during those war years. While in the duplex, I have memories of playing with my cousin, Geri Roth (Jacobson) and of going to the movies with our mothers. I also recall playing at Marian Ullman's house and cutting my leg on a tin can that left a long scar for years. (I just tried to find the scar and it looks like it disappeared, but I do remember that this really happened.)

Stanley Papel circa 1943

Stanley Papel circa 1945

I was born with a rather large red birthmark on my left forearm. It was a growing mass of red blood vessels which the doctor recommended removing by using dry ice treatments. These occurred from the age of 8 months old until I reached the age of 3 years. The result was a flattened, large, scarred area that measured approximately 2-1/2 inches in diameter. Today it barely shows since the area is covered by hair and has faded to skin color, but I remember being somewhat sensitive about it as a child. My baby pictures all have the area covered by a stuffed animal or my parents covering up the area with their hands. I am told that my parents would take me to the doctor and my father used to have to hold me down while the doctor administered the painful dry ice treatment. I screamed whenever I saw doctors in white coats as a reaction to the fear from the painful treatments. I remember going on a streetcar with my mom to give the doctor a beautiful gift set of cards and poker chips as a "thank you" for treating the birthmark after he completed all the treatments. Today, I understand that raised blood vessels of the type I was born with are not treated and disappear naturally in time.

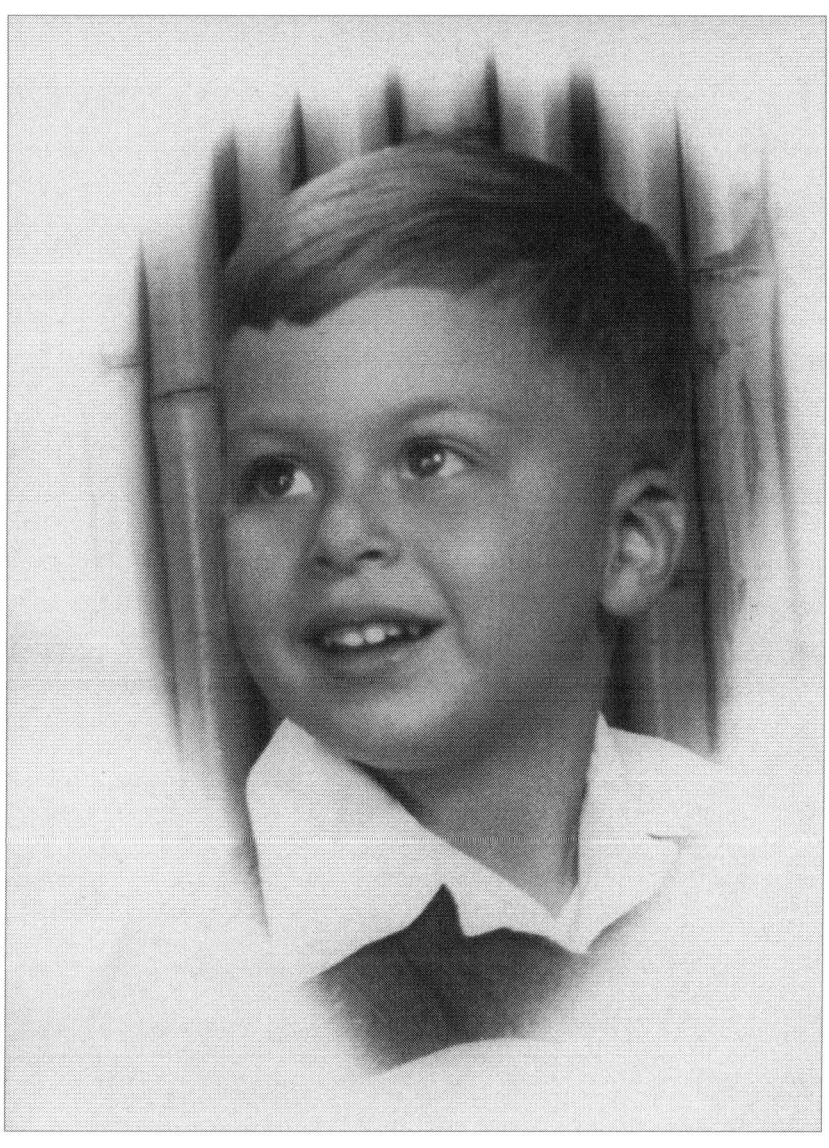

Stanley Papel circa 1946

Among my other early childhood memories, one stands out in particular. My cousin Geraldine Roth lived on 5th Avenue, the block next to me. I was very close to her, and my mom would bring me over to see her and visit my grandmother. Geri and I would play together and sometimes go to the movies at the Forum Theater (the admission price was only ten cents in those days). After the movies, I would buy a treat, which was a packaged type of chocolate cake with a delicious white cream filling that cost a nickel. Anyway, my memory is of a "bad" lady who lived a couple of doors away from the Roth's. We were told not to talk to her. However, Geri and I would always say, "hi" to her and she would respond back, "Hi, you old kike." I asked my mom what a kike was and she said that it is a bad way of calling someone Jewish. I must have been three-years old at the time, but the memory stands out in my mind very vividly. I will ask my cousin Geri if she remembers this, but I doubt it since she is a year younger than I am. I also recollect at age 3 or 4 going into my parents' closet at the duplex and discovering a big box of neat, white things that looked to me like shoulder pads. My mom explained to me that she used them for her monthly cycle, leaving me very much intrigued with my discovery.

The rest of my early childhood memories revolve around our moving from the duplex near my grandmother's house to my parents' first new home at 2520 Butler Avenue in West Los Angeles. That move took place in 1946 and I was only 3 ½ years old. We lived at that home until I was ten years old, and then we moved to what was my parents' dream home at 517 Cashmere Terrace, where incidentally my sister and her family live today. The home on Butler was obtained using some type of veteran's benefit that my dad earned for his service in the war. My dad told me that the home cost $11,000, which was considered a very good deal then. Before moving there, I remember my dad and his close friend, Jack Levin, sneaking into the house with me one evening. My dad explained that since we did not own the house we were not supposed to be there, but he wanted to see the inside again. Because it had turned dark, he and Jack had flashlights as we walked through the empty house. Later we visited what was to be Jack and Shiffra's house, located only a few blocks away. Jack and Shiffra were my parents' closest friends throughout my childhood years. Not having any children, they were like second parents to me and my sister. I was especially fond of Shiffra and loved her very much as I know she loved me. She had the funniest sense of humor and was a totally genuine and sweet person, just like my mom. I still cannot think about her without feeling a loss as she passed away at a young age after much suffering.

The big event at the new house occurred on September 7, 1947, with the birth of my sister, Arlene. I remember being dropped off at my grandparents Effie and Mike's home and being told that very soon I would have a new brother or sister. I was ecstatic to see my little sister and looked forward very much to becoming a big brother.

CHAPTER 2

STANLEY PAPEL
FAMILY AND FRIENDS (1947–1952)

I was fortunate to have both of my grandmothers living into my adult years. My first memories of Bubbe and Grandpa Joe are from their home in Boyle Heights on City Terrace, which is the house where my dad was raised. I remember the garage that housed their home-based business, "Ever Art Ceramics," along with the neighborhood that included the apartment house where my Uncle Sol and Aunt Sonya lived.

This may sound funny, but as a young child, I did not realize that Bubbe was my grandmother. I thought "Bubbe" was her first name and that she was a woman living with my Grandpa Joe. When I was probably about 6 years old, they moved to Alhambra, and only then did discover that Bubbe was also my grandmother.

Bubbe was a dynamic woman—a real pistol! She could be your best friend or your worst enemy. Fortunately, we were always best friends, but I felt sorry for anyone who ever crossed her. She definitely wore the pants in that family. I remember my Grandpa Joe as always being very easy going and doing whatever Bubbe told him. Sometimes she would get upset with him and from that I learned a few choice words of Yiddish which I should not repeat here.

I remember the family get-togethers on my dad's side of the family. My dad had three brothers: Sol, Bernie and Sid and a sister, Mary. Uncle Bernie was the "black sheep" and did not attend many of the family gatherings. I was especially fond of Aunt Mary and my cousin Rochelle (Ricki), who was Sol's daughter. Bubbe was the one who held the family together. When she died, there were seldom any occasions for the family to get together. My dad and his brother Sid were very close. But my father's family is not really close any more.

When my parents took vacations, Bubbe and Grandpa Joe would stay at our home and take care of Arlene and me. Grandpa Joe would always "miss the toilet" and would cause my Bubbe to yell in Yiddish. With all the arguing, I was glad when my parents came home.

One really funny thing (not so funny at the time) happened at Bubbe's 80th birthday party. Dinner was catered at a restaurant and the entire family was there to celebrate. As we assembled, it became evident that the honored guest was not there. Everyone had assumed that someone else was going to pick up Bubbe. Needless to say, the party started later than planned, and we had one angry Bubbe to deal with. Happily, the evening ended up being a wonderful event.

My Grandpa Joe died in 1964. Bubbe lived alone for many more years until she died in 1982. Bubbe did mellow in her later years and her inner sweetness became much more apparent. When I go through difficult times, I always come out a "survivor." I think I get that fighting spirit and inner strength from Bubbe.

I also have a very special place in my heart for my Grandma Effie. Having lived in her home from infancy through age three created a special bond like a child feels towards his mother. Grandma Effie was certainly more reserved than Bubbe, but she also had a way of "getting her point across."

Grandma Effie always made a big secret of her age. I was curious how old she was, but she would never tell me. It was not until she died that I finally found out her age, but by then it did not seem that important to me.

Grandma Effie had a few favorite phrases she would use frequently. She would never swear and would have substitute wording. For example, she would say, "cheese and crackers, got all muddy." Can you figure out what that stood for? She would also say, "It's raining cats and dogs, I just stepped in a poodle." Funny, the things that stand out in your mind.

When Grandma Effie got old and frail, she deteriorated as had Bubbe before dying. She reached a point when she could no longer speak. The last time I saw her before she died, she squeezed my finger. I knew exactly what she was saying to me; she was telling me she could no longer speak, but that she loved me. She was also saying goodbye to me.

Grandma Effie died shortly after my son Evan was born. So, Evan was named after his great grandmother, which was unusual since she was still alive at the time that he was born. Although she could not speak, I introduced him to her as her new great-grandson. She reached out her hand and touched Evan with love. I read her mind as she was saying in her thoughts, "I am passing my life on through you."

Both Grandma Effie and Bubbe also had a deep love for my daughter Melissa, although I know Melissa does not remember them except through pictures. I wish that my other daughter Dara had been able to meet her great grandmas. Dara has a lot of Bubbe's spirit in her.

During my elementary school days at Richland Avenue School, I was very close with all of my cousins on my mom's side of the family, even closer than my sister Arlene, due to her being younger. We all lived very close to each other; my cousins Bobby and Carole Leff lived next door. Janet and David Ullman lived within a mile, as did Geri and Marc Roth. Cousins Marian Ullman and Stephanie Leff were like sisters to my mom and were also very close with her brother Larry Roth.

We even formed a "Cousins Club" consisting of all the cousins except for David Ullman, who was three years older than me and did not want to be with the younger kids. Janet Ullman is six months younger than me. Geri Roth is a year younger. Once, the Cousins Club made "adobe bricks" which were nothing more than mud pies.

I remember when we got our first television set, the first in the neighborhood. I was so excited as my dad was having it installed that I danced a jig around the room. However, I slipped on the packaging and banged my head on the TV, with my laughter quickly changing into tears. Later, I would anxiously await the weekly Milton Berle Show as well as my other favorites, Howdy Doody and my hero Flash Gordon.

At Richland Avenue School, there were carnivals each semester. Once we went without my parents, and I was responsible for taking care of Arlene. I was with my cousins, and we all wanted to sit in the bleachers. However, Arlene was afraid to go up too high for fear of falling through the space between the seat and the foot area. I told her not to be a "scaredy cat." Well, I don't know how, but she fell through the bleachers onto the ground. It is probably her first memory of me, and she has reminded me several times over the years of it.

Once when were on a family vacation, we passed by a factory. Arlene asked what they were making there, and I replied, "That's where they manufacture clouds." Well, I forgot to tell her I was joking, and I think she was nearly in college before she found out that clouds were not manufactured in factories. Speaking of naivete, I was already in college before I found that "tushy" was not an English word. We used "tushy" so often at home that I really thought it was in the English language.

I had lots of friends in the neighborhood when we lived at Butler Avenue. Because I did well in school, I was advanced one semester higher. I did not care for this much, as I preferred to be with the kids my own age and did not like being younger than most of the other kids in the classroom.

My best friend when I lived on Butler Avenue was Randy Carter. I cannot exactly remember when he moved away, but I did keep in touch with him for a while after we moved. The other good friend I had on Butler was Pamela Hall, who lived across the street. Pamela picked her nose and saved her boogers on the wall next to her bed. She would show me this massive collection of dried boogers that probably represented several years of accumulation. She is probably a very dignified 60-plus year-old lady today and would never admit to the wall of boogers.

One last memory before I close the chapter on Butler Avenue is that my sister and I shared a bedroom. (The house was probably about 1200 square feet consisting of two bedrooms and a den.) Arlene wanted to go to bed at the same time as me, which I did not think was fair since I was 4 1/2 years older. So there would be a ritual every night. We would go into the bedroom at the same time, and I would say, "I'm going to sleep, and I'm not going to talk to you." Mom would come and tuck me in and give me a good night kiss. Then she would tuck Arlene in and lean over her to give her a good night kiss. After Mom did this, I would position the pillows to look like my body and sneak out of the bedroom in order to stay up another hour or so.

I want to tell about an event that was traumatic to me as a young lad. I do not blame my parents because in those days, the mindset was different than today. At age five, I went to a sleep-away camp for three weeks. Today, parents wait until children are older for camp, but in those days, it was common. Those three weeks at Camp Kiowa were pure hell for me, and I am sure impacted my self-esteem for years to come.

I was the youngest in my cabin, and when I started crying because I missed my mom, I was called "baby." I became the target of everyone in the cabin and was picked on and bullied. I remember being hit, ostracized, and in my mind, tortured to the point of silently crying myself to sleep every night. The counselor was of no help. The only friend I had was the camp nurse. I begged my parents to take me home, but I was told it was necessary to stick out the three weeks.

My parents' close friends, Earl and Elaine Himovitz, also sent their son, Freddy, to the same camp though he was assigned to a different cabin. I tried to pal around with him, but he told me that he could not be my friend at camp because, if he were, the other kids would not like him. My parents remained close friends with his parents, but I lost respect for him that day for his conforming to peer pressure rather than doing what he was felt was the right thing to do.

My father had become successful in business by the time I was midway through elementary school. He was sales manager for Ever Art Ceramics, which meant he had to travel a lot during the year. I believe some of his trips were as long as six weeks, as he called on major accounts throughout the country and exhibited in gift shows. Sometimes he would take me on business trips with him that were relatively short. I remember having to wait in the car while he called on accounts, and I hated sitting there waiting for what seemed like hours (but in reality, it was not).

My dad made strong efforts to bond with me during this time. He tried hard to be my pal as well as my father. But I remember being resentful of him. In retrospect, I think it was due to his inconsistent presence during those formative years. Even so, I know my dad eventually ended his career with Ever Art so that he could spend more time with my mom, my sister, and me.

As a child, I remember our many family vacations. We used to spend a week in Balboa every summer, renting the same place each time. We customarily went with two other families: the Slaffs and Jack and Shiffra Levin. My dad enjoyed filming the family vacations and other events, and they were eventually compiled into silent eight-millimeter films. Some of my favorite vacations were at Las Vegas (where I would sneak and play the slot machines whenever possible) and at Camp Curry in Yosemite Park.

Stanley and Arlene Papel circa 1950

CHAPTER 3

STANLEY PAPEL
SCHOOL YEARS (1952–1967)

The person I was closest to during my childhood was definitely my mother. I have always thought of her, and still do, as the kindest, most loving person in the world. I do not think there is a mean bone in my mother's body, and she gave unconditional love and support to my father, my sister, and me. My dad was the disciplinarian in my family. If I was bad, my mom said she would tell my father.

When I was 10 years old, we moved to the house my parents had built on Cashmere Terrace in the Brentwood area of Los Angeles. It was their dream house, which they designed to contain many features that they wanted. There was a storage closet hidden behind a wall, a walk-in bar, a built-in barbecue, and I remember a revolving cupboard in the kitchen that housed my mom's pots and pans. I actually would crawl into that closet and hide sometimes. I had my own bedroom with built-in bookshelves and a bulletin board above my desk. I also had a secret place below my bottom drawer where I used to hide my coin collections. When we moved, it was in the middle of a semester, so I felt very much alone, arriving mid-year at my new school in Brentwood. However, I soon made new friends, including Bernie Kamins, who I still regard and love as a brother. I lived at Cashmere Terrace from the fifth grade until my first year at college, and I am glad the home now belongs to my sister Arlene.

In 1955, my dad opened Ruggles China and Gift shop in Disneyland. During the school year, my dad would drive over an hour each way to Anaheim and back home. He used to complain about the commute, something I really did not appreciate until I was much older. I took it for granted that this was what he was supposed to do. Beginning in the summer of 1955 we moved to a second home in Garden Grove during the summer, so that my dad did not have to make the drive during the busy season when he worked even longer hours. We relocated to Orange County every summer until my sophomore year of college. I remember disliking the summer moves since all my other friends were doing fun things in Brentwood while we would have to be in Garden Grove. The first summer in 1955, we had an apartment, but thereafter my parents bought a home on Morgan Lane, which became our second home and was reminiscent of the house on Butler Avenue.

I worked at Ruggles in Disneyland each day during the summer and was a very good at what I did. I was fast at the cash register, which I preferred over selling. When it was not busy,

I would also look through coins and was able to put together a very good coin collection. At one time, I had every Lincoln cent to date, some of which I had to buy, including a 1909 SVDB in extra fine condition. My dad would also bring rolls of pennies and nickels for me to go through in my spare time at home. After many summers of working at Ruggles, I built up a good bank account for a kid of my age. I remember I had enough money from my earnings to buy anything I really wanted that was not part of my allowance. Much of my extra savings went into purchasing coins or proof sets. They ended up being gleaming investments when I finally sold them in the 1970's when silver hit $40 an ounce. I am sure I also gained good business experience during those summers, so although I did not appreciate it at the time, the summers were far from a waste.

My best friend Bernie Kamins lived right around the corner from me in Brentwood and, besides being in many classes together in school, we shared activities in camp, social clubs, and even double dated. Once we even dated twins and then "switched" after several dates. On another double date we gave corsages to our dates. However, it turned out that the florist charged extra for each corsage box. Therefore, we decided to get just one box and re-use it. Bernie gave the corsage first, so he had to ask his date for the box back and then he secretly slipped it to me.

One summer at camp in Malibu, Bernie and I were hiking somewhere on our own. All of a sudden, Bernie started screaming and started running in many directions. My first thought was that he had finally gone crazy. Well, suddenly I felt pain like my head was splitting open. I also started screaming and running after Bernie. I realized we were being stung by a hive of bees that were chasing us. We ran directly to the nurse's office. She promptly poured a bottle of bleach on our heads and pulled the stingers out. Bernie and I also went to camp one summer in Catalina, another camping experience I enjoyed.

I was always a good student in school, receiving high grades and studying very hard. I did not think of myself as especially intelligent. What I did know is that I had to be good in something, so then I would work hard in school in order to achieve high grades. I was not good in sports, something I was very sensitive about as a child. In the neighborhood, none of the kids wanted me to play with them because I was so lousy. In school, when they chose teams in gym class, I was always one of the last kids to be selected, which brought back the feelings of inadequacy of my Camp Kiowa days. Rather than try to improve at things I struggled with, I worked harder at the things I could excel in, such as academics. I can see that this tendency continued into my adult years, although after my eye surgery in 1981-1982, I finally took some steps to get into good physical condition.

I transferred schools again at the end of the fifth grade since a new school, Bel Air Elementary, opened closer to home. I ran for school president in the sixth grade and came in second place. That was my lone foray into politics.

I attended Emerson Junior High near Westwood Village from 7th to 9th grade. My middle school years were rather uneventful except that my hormones started working. My favorite class was math, physical education was not enjoyable, and my Latin course was difficult. At that time, some kids would take classes in "ballroom dancing." I participated in the popular Ted Raden dance classes, and I was considered to be a very good dancer. In some ways that made up for not being very good at physical education.

On December 17, 1955, I turned 13. For a good Jewish boy, it means a Bar Mitzvah service followed by a celebration party. Foreign languages were never my forte, so reading in Hebrew from the Torah was not easy for me, and I never really understood what I was reciting. However, I had very good coaching from the Cantor for about a year. I think I did a good job and gave a decent speech—in English. I actually still have the tape recording of the service. We had been members of Reformed University Synagogue in West Los Angeles from its earliest days, and my dad was somewhat active in the congregation and friendly with Rabbi Feingold.

After the service there was a party held at the Carolina Pines, one of the better restaurants in West Hollywood at the time. Through the many photos I have of the event, I can recollect much of the day and evening. There was a table of my friends, including Bernie Kamins and Alex Waugh, who are still my best friends today.

My hobbies were an important part of my spare time when I was growing up. First, there was coin collecting, which I did with a passion. At that time, it was possible to find valuable and semi-valuable coins in circulation. Sometimes, in one day, I would go through rolls and rolls of coins from my dad's store, trying to find the good dates. When I would find a good date, it was like hitting the jackpot!

I also enjoyed raising fish in aquariums. I started with one aquarium of tropical fish and ended up breeding them with several aquariums all over the house. I know my mom was not too thrilled about aquariums in the bathrooms, bedrooms, and especially spread out on her buffet in our dining room. Nevertheless, she was always a good sport in letting me pursue my hobbies—except when fish jumped out of the tank, and we would find dead, dried-out tropical fish on the corners of the buffet.

Once when we moved to Garden Grove during the summer, I took the fish with me. I got a wading pool and kept them outside for the summer. Then at the end of the summer, I took them out of the pool, but I guess the algae and temperature changes affected the fish. They had grown larger and become very scaly. I remember they looked like mutants.

My other hobby was collecting 45 rpm records. Recent generations might not know what they were, but that is how young people listened to music before CD's and streaming. My uncle Morris Piltzer had given me a large jukebox that took up half of my bedroom which I could play the records on. When I was in high school, each Thursday, Bernie and I would go to a liquor store that had obtained used records from jukeboxes and resold them for 25 cents each. We would rush there in order to be the first to choose from their recent arrivals. I divided my bulletin board with labels showing the "Top Ten for the Week," and then I mathematically would re-calculate and show the "Top Ten for the Month" and "Top Ten for the Year." Unfortunately, I sold a good part of my record collection at a garage sale. I had many of the top hits of the 1950's, starting with "Rock Around the Clock."

As I think about my hobbies, I suddenly recall my first big hobby, which was trading collector cards. I started collecting them when I lived on Butler Avenue and continued for many years. I had thousands of cards and had the best collection of "pin-ups" in town. I kept the collection in my parents' storage wall and years later, when I was in college and went to retrieve them, the cards were gone! Only recently did I learn that my mom had thrown them out, thinking that I no longer wanted them.

In high school, I dated quite a lot, especially once I had a car at age 16. My parents had bought my Aunt Hattie's '51 Chevy that was to be my car for several years and ran like a fine watch. I did not belong to any clubs except for the AZA., a social group for Jewish boys. It had "socials" with the BBG (B'nai B'rith Girls). How times have changed! Anyway, I met many girls at the BBG socials. Being a good dancer and owning a car made the dating process smooth and a lot of fun.

Sometimes I dated several different girls at the same time and other times I dated primarily one girl, although I never formally went "steady" while I was in high school or college. Before getting married, I threw away "my little black book" which contained the names and number of more than 100 girls. That surprised even me.

My high school years at University High from 1957 to 1960 were not particularly happy. I was a very good student and had very high grades. However, at the time, what seemed important was being "popular" and having a "personality." However, I lacked confidence in those areas.

My time of excelling, growing and having a good time was in my college years. I should first explain that I went to seven colleges between 1960 to 1964, before receiving my Bachelor of Arts in Psychology. Although it may sound crazy to have gone to so many colleges, I would not have changed anything about my college experience. I actually graduated in 3 ½ years and went on to get my MBA at UCLA after completing some work experience.

Having accumulated a good grade point average in high school, I had my choice of colleges. Some of my friends were going to University of California, Berkeley, or Santa Barbara, but the truth is that I chose UCLA because I felt like I was not quite ready to leave home yet. My traumatic Camp Kiowa experience was something that was still affecting me. I would not have attended the other camps that I went to without the comfort of having my friend Bernie Kamins.

I started at UCLA, an apprehensive, undecided freshman, and I enrolled in 15 units. One of my classes was Psychology 1A, which I thoroughly enjoyed. It impressed me so much that it led to my decision to major in psychology. Although I was uncertain whether I wanted to be a psychologist, I immensely enjoyed the classes in my major along with the majority of my other courses.

The summer before enrolling at UCLA, as usual, we moved to Orange County. Since Santa Ana Junior College was close by, I took English 1A and a political science course to get some classes out of the way.

My friend Bernie told me how great it was at UCSB, and by the time I finished my first year, I felt confident enough to decide on a move to Santa Barbara for my sophomore year. Then, I would decide whether to stay at UCSB or transfer back to UCLA.

In the summer preceding my enrollment at UCSB, I was back in Orange County working at Disneyland as well as taking classes at both Santa Ana Junior College and Orange Coast College. At the time of my transfer to UCSB, it was a relatively small university with only 4,000 students. The campus was converted from a World War II army base. The dorm that I stayed in was an old army barrack. I was told I shared the best room because hidden behind the mirror was a clandestine bar where I could hide any number of wine bottles.

I did make some nice friends at Santa Barbara, and one night right before classes started, we decided to go bowling (the campus was located in Goleta about 10 miles from Santa Barbara). I ended up being hit with a bowling ball above my left eye requiring several stitches and resulting in a massive black eye. I also ended up getting a terrible cold and could hardly talk. When my parents came to visit me one week after I moved out, they saw their little boy's face adorned in black and blue, sick, and unable to speak. My mom took me in her arms and started to cry.

After going to a big school like UCLA, I was not too impressed with the classes or choices at a smaller college. My roommate, Roland Lynn, and I became close friends and we decided to transfer to Berkeley during the second part of our sophomore year. I had pretty much decided that after attending U.C. Berkeley for a time, I would return to UCLA during my junior year and finish up with my B.A. in Psychology. Roland passed away very young but even today I keep in touch with his wife, Gail Lynn.

I enjoyed U.C. Berkeley very much. I lived in the new dorms, sharing the room with Roland. I enjoyed the classes and made new friends. I handled a full load of units, but wanted to make money, so I took my first job (outside of family positions) at the cafeteria as "Dessert Boy." My job was to keep the rows filled with dessert, scoop the ice cream, and to be responsible for keeping the glasses filled and lined up with lemonade and iced tea. It was not long before I had a system going and could easily keep up with the line of hungry customers. I think I was carrying up to six or seven pieces of pie at once and did not drop a single pie in my career as dessert boy.

However, I did have one experience that I will remember for all of my life! When the large canisters of lemonade and iced tea were low, I was supposed to go into this large walk-in refrigerator and refill them. We did this by turning on the lever on these enormous tubs that I am sure held more than 100 gallons each.

Once, seeing that both the lemonade and iced tea were both empty at the same time, I took both vats into the walk-in refrigerator at the same time to be refilled. I turned on the lemonade, and rather than wait for it to fill, I left it on. I then walked to the iced tea vat and turned that one on. I waited for the iced tea vat to fill, but it must have contained less volume than the lemonade and came out slower because when the iced tea was filled, I turned it off, and walked over to the lemonade. To my astonishment, the lemonade had come out quicker and was overflowing with gallons having spilled all over the entire refrigerator floor. I was horrified, to say the least, and on the verge of tears. I had to tell the boss what happened and was afraid I would be fired. She understood and I believe she had someone mop it up while I returned to my station. Later, I was offered more hours and more pay, but had to decline the promotion. At least my first job at school turned out to be a successful experience, even with the lemonade fiasco.

With my savings from the cafeteria job and my parent's sponsorship, I did a summer program at the University of Hawaii in 1962. I took six units which consisted of courses in psychology and economics. My classes each day concluded before 11 AM, giving me plenty of time to study at the beach.

That was a great summer beginning with the "economy class" cruise. Thirty people shared a room on a major cruise ship consisting primarily of students. It was a five-day voyage from Los Angeles to Hawaii for $80 and included three meals a day and lavish parties all night.

At the end of the six weeks of classes, my parents and Arlene flew over for a family vacation on Oahu and Kauai. Arlene was in high school and some of my friends were finding her attractive. I think that was the first time I realized that my sister was not a little girl anymore.

After the summer, I started back at UCLA, but there was a problem. Although I had accumulated many units, I never completed a foreign language requirement. I needed to complete 12 units by the end of my junior year. Foreign languages were always a difficult subject for me, and I thought maybe if I started a new language, everything would be okay. Therefore, I enrolled in Danish during my junior year. That lasted about one week when I realized everyone in the class had Danish origins and knew more than I did.

Therefore, I dropped out of college and got a job as a clerk at the UCLA Job Placement Center. It turned out to be a very good job, and I was quickly promoted to a full-time interviewer-level job, making $2.65 an hour (minimum scale was then $1.00 an hour). The job also allowed me the chance to take numerous temporary high paying jobs, like playing Pan against experts in an experiment at the Friars Club. However, my parents put their feet down when I was about to accept being an experimental subject for a new mind-altering drug called LSD. I did end up working at the placement center part-time in my senior and post-graduate years.

In the winter of 1963, I decided to complete my foreign language requirement at the University of America in Mexico City. I could take in two quarters of all the units required for the foreign language requirement. Further, I could "live the language" while having a chance to know my relatives, the Weinstocks, who lived in Mexico City. I had become confident as a traveler, and this seemed like a natural way to complete the foreign language requirement. Initially, I stayed with my wonderful family there, Willy and Rosa Weinstock, whom I adopted as my Mexican Mama and Papa. Then, I moved into a large house sharing the third story of the quarters with about five other students. Finally, during the 1963 spring quarter, I shared an apartment that was a luxury and a bargain.

My senior year was spent at UCLA, and I received my bachelor's degree in 1964. That is the story of my seven colleges with my MBA being relatively dull, but stable, from UCLA.

Although I had a feeling I would eventually work in my father's business, I wanted a break from school as well as the opportunity to get some work experience. Having worked at the UCLA Student and Alumni Placement Center, I knew the interview process of major companies coming to campus. This knowledge facilitated obtaining a position as a loan officer in a training program with Bank of America. The pay was not great, but $700 a month was not bad either for 1964 for an inexperienced college graduate.

I knew that I would not make a career in banking, and I figured getting the financial background would be helpful regardless of where I finally settled in a career. For several months, I went from branch to branch learning different functions. During training, I was at a branch for a few weeks, but after training was completed I had my first position at the bank's Gower and Sunset branch in Hollywood. I did not like the bank or that area of the city. I handled installment loans and called on past due accounts. About the funniest thing that happened there was related to another loan officer by the name of Donald Duck, believe it or not. He would make these phone calls stating, "This is Donald Duck and I'm calling about your past due loan." I could not help but laugh aloud every time he made those calls.

I remember there were dress standards like white shirt and tie. It bothered me to feel I had to conform to the company in not only the way I dressed, but also the way I acted. I knew if I had ever decided to make a career at that bank, my livelihood and lifestyle would be very mediocre.

Still, the experience was worthwhile and when a new branch opened (I was not selected to work there), I informed them that I was stepping down and decided to go back to school and get my master's degree. I left the door open to returning to work with them, stating that I would be more valuable to the bank with an advance degree. I also worked part-time at the Sunset and La Cienega branch while getting my MBA. I knew that I would never return to banking once I obtained my MBA.

I remember that going back to school seemed a little strange after working for more than a year. Getting back into the mode of studying was not too difficult, but I had liked in some ways the working life and it seemed a step backward to be in school again.

I already had taken several business and economic classes as an undergraduate, so I did not have to take the full 60 units for the MBA. The field of concentration I specialized in was marketing. Within that field, I studied "Consumer Behavior," which was a blend of business administration and psychology. Therefore, with my MBA in hand in the summer of 1967, I was ready to conquer the world!

The transition though between graduate school and the working world culminated with a once-in-a-lifetime 3 ½-month trip to Europe and Israel during the fall of 1967.

Incredibly, I really did do Europe on $5 a day (excluding plane fare). I went with a friend, David Brown, and we met another fellow along the way, so we shared hotel and gas expenses between the three of us. David had purchased a Volkswagen, so for a good part of the trip we drove until he had it shipped back to Greece. We started in the United Kingdom, where we met my cousin, Nancy Rand (Nancy Koopersmith), who I have been close to ever since. I am not sure, but I remember visiting the United Kingdom, Netherlands, Belgium, Denmark, Germany, Austria, Italy, Yugoslavia, Cypress, Greece, and Israel.

One thing I will never forget is that my friend David had claustrophobia, and he became more and more difficult to be with. On the flight to Israel, a small student-chartered plane, we made an intermediary stop in Cypress, and David got up from his seat and left the plane. I thought he had to go to the bathroom, but it turned out he had panicked and ran right past the immigration officers in Cypress. Being right after the Six-Day War in 1967 and time of high tension, they thought he might have planted a bomb on the plane. They questioned me because I was with him and removed our luggage for a complete inspection. David finally arrived in Israel about five days later by boat, and then he returned home on a larger plane.

Israel was especially meaningful to me. It was as if everyone was my relative, and for the first time I really felt my Jewish identity.

My final stop was in New York in what I believe was December 1967. It felt good to be back in the USA. In those three months, I had shed 30 pounds going from 160 to 131. Although I had eaten very well, I probably lost all my baby fat. I left all my travel clothes in New York, as even Goodwill would not have wanted them at that point. So, bound with my one new clean outfit, I flew home to Los Angeles to start my life as a working man.

*Bellagio Rd Elementary School (Graduating Class in 1954).
Bottom Row L-R= #6 Alex Waugh, #11 Bernie Kamins.
Middle Row= #3 Stanley Papel*

Stanley Papel. Bar Mitzvah in 1955

Stanley Papel. University High School Graduation in 1960

Stanley Papel. UCLA Graduation in 1964

CHAPTER 4

Stanley Papel
BACHELOR DAYS (1967–1972)

Having an MBA provided greater career opportunities than when I only had a bachelor's degree. In 1967, there were many more jobs available for people with MBA's than there were graduates, so most MBA graduates could pick and choose from several offers.

I had known in my heart that my best opportunity would be in the family business. Dad really wanted me to go into the business, and it was becoming very strong in the retail trade. Ruggles Gifts already had several retail locations, and the wholesale division, Phil Papel Imports, was starting to grow. On the other hand, neither my dad nor mom wanted me to go into the family business as an obligation. Also, I had reservations about beginning my career by working with Dad right out of school. I wanted to prove to myself that I could make a career for myself and succeed without the opportunity handed to me "on a silver platter."

With that in mind, the job that seemed the best to me was a special training program offered by the May Company that was just being initiated. It was offered to three MBA's. Each would serve as an assistant to one of the three vice presidents of merchandising. While May Company had a general program, this new one seemed to be a perfect opportunity for me to work directly with someone knowledgeable and successful in the company. The job paid $14,000 per year, which was very competitive in those days. It was also quite a step up from the $800 per month I had been earning at Bank of America prior to going into business school at UCLA.

I was assigned to Leo Pollakoff, Vice President of Merchandising of the Budget Stores of the May Company. This division of the company handled all the lower priced merchandise. There were 18 branches of May Company at the time, and they all had budget stores.

I worked out of the company's main office in downtown Los Angeles. One of my responsibilities included assigning the "bargain booths" to the buyers. These buyers were quite competitive about wanting a good location to maximize sales at each booth, so I took the responsibility very seriously. I found out what each buyer projected he or she would sell if I assigned them one of the better booths. My other responsibility was coordinating the advertising for the budget stores. On Wednesdays, I would visit the branches and learn a lot from the criticisms made by the General Merchandise Manager, Mr. Pollakoff, and the two Divisional Merchandise managers, Mr. Ira Ginsberg, and the crazy Mr. Flicker.

After several months, I was moved from my training position to a permanent position as Associate Buyer of the Cosmetics Department under a longtime buyer, Mr. Jim Gilhooley. The Divisional Merchandise Manager that I worked under, Mr. Henry Sulzberger, had also been with the May Company for a long time. Both men were wonderful teachers and were to become closer friends well after my time with the May Company.

I was a hard worker, which turned out to be an advantage because Mr. Gilhooley had gone through many assistant buyers, perhaps because they did not demonstrate a strong work ethic. I was his first "associate" buyer, and he showed a respect for me that he had never shown to previous assistants. We went to New York quite often together, "wining and dining" with clients in the cosmetics industry, being courted by the likes of Revlon, Shiseido, and Max Factor. Incidentally, our cosmetics department had sales of more than $8 million per year, the largest in the company. I considered myself as very fortunate to have this position.

One recollection was the wig-mania that started in about 1969 and which increased our sales tremendously. We retailed Deltress wigs at $11.99, which would sell as fast as we could put them on the shelves. There were at least 30 different shades, which I knew by memory. Women would grab them out of my hands when I would personally replenish the inventory. We would fly the re-orders in from England, where they were manufactured. Later, there would be more competition in the wigs market, but as Mr. Sulzberger told me, "a hot one like this comes once, if ever, for a buyer," so I should enjoy the success of it. As much as I liked May Company and the people I worked with, I always knew that I would eventually join my dad's company, and I hoped that I would be able to experience a success like this in the family business.

My parents owned two apartment buildings in West Los Angeles. I lived at and managed their building at 1850 Camden Avenue #4 through 1972 when Aileen and I were married. While still a bachelor, however, this was a great "bachelor pad." It was a furnished two-bedroom with a very nice patio. I did not have any roommates, although I remember Bernie stayed with me for a short time. My future wife Aileen was with me in the apartment when the major earthquake of 1970 struck Los Angeles. We were both working at the May Company at that time, and when we went to work a couple of days later, parts of the building were damaged badly.

While on the subject of apartments, I remember the two apartments that I lived in as a graduate student at UCLA. Both were in West Los Angeles, one on Armacost Avenue, the other on Ohio Avenue in a complex called the "Roman Gardens." I shared a spacious one-bedroom apartment with two roommates (and a cat that I did not care for much). One of my roommates, Shigeru Matsui, from Japan became a lifetime friend. I still correspond every Christmas with him and his wife Yuko. Once Aileen and I visited them in Japan, and they visited us in the United States.

My term of employment with the May Company came to an end in 1970, when Dad made me an irresistible offer to become part of the family business. I felt the timing was right for me to make the career change since Dad had already offered my high school friend, Dick Saklad, a position in the wholesale company with an ownership option and was considering a similar request from another key employee. Besides, Dad had received the rights to operate the souvenir concessions aboard the Queen Mary, which was going to be permanently docked in Long Beach. Dad said if I came into the company at that point, I could own 100% of Ruggles/

QM Inc., for which he would capitalize a starting amount. That offer seemed right for me. During the time I had worked at the May Company, I had a strong interest in the retail side of the business. Even though my dad had lost his store in Disneyland, he still had many other successful retail stores at the Disneyland Hotel, in Century City and Oceanside, and three at Ports of Call Village in San Pedro.

When I gave notice to the May Company, they were very disappointed to lose me. The top management had told me I was in line for promotions and that I was positioned to be eventually in upper management if I continued my excellent performance. I had used a formula for myself of always doing more than was required or expected. For example, I had done on my own a very comprehensive analysis of the cosmetic department by product category with suggestions of methods and directions that would improve sales. I know the report made its way up the ladder when the president of the May Company, Howard Goldfeder, invited me to lunch in order to ask me to reconsider my decision. It was one of the highest compliments in my career. However, I still felt the opportunity with a family business was best, and had accomplished my personal goal of knowing that I could be successful on my own.

My dad's business was quite small when I started. The wholesale division, Phil Papel Imports (PPI as it was called), did less than $500,000 per year. The retail stores did more volume, probably under $1,000,000 per year. Applying my Business Administration education to it, I found the business to be unstructured and lacking policies and procedures. Due to my experience at the May Company I felt there needed to be immediate changes in the way things were handled in the office. For example, receiving records were not kept and checks were signed without backup documentation. The result was that invoices were often paid twice. Dad was a great salesperson and Dick Saklad learned salesmanship from my dad; however, no one was properly overseeing the purchasing or accounting records. Also, since the office and warehouse had recently relocated from Anaheim to South Central Los Angeles, most of the staff was carpooling into work from Orange County.

My dad was supportive of me and told the women in the office that I was now in charge. They did not like the change from Dad's and Dick's easygoing ways. I cannot remember if Thelma, the bookkeeper resigned or I terminated her, but I quickly replaced her with Mack Iwamoto, who I knew from the May Company. It was nice to have someone I could trust working with me at the time.

Now let me turn to my love life at the time. The year was 1971, and my sister had been dating Jay Slater whom she met at the May Company. My cousin Carole Leff had just recently gotten married, and my cousins Geri Roth and Janet Ullman had married several years earlier. My friends were all getting married, and I was tired of playing around. I was considered a good catch, so I was not having any problems finding dates, but I was often lonesome and felt ready to settle down and have a family if I could ever find the right girl. I was dating several girls, some I knew from my twenties. Probably my closest girlfriend was Barbara Katz, who I actually knew from junior high school and continued a friendship with throughout the years. I was seeing one girl for quite a while, and we became briefly engaged. When I say "briefly," that is exactly what I mean. We were engaged and disengaged within 24 hours! After accepting, she told me that it just was not "right" and that she was not ready to be married. In looking back, I do not think our marriage would have lasted. Although my pride was hurt, it was the right decision.

Then something very special happened. I met Aileen Miller on July 20, 1971. My dad had taken his tuxedo to his tailor, Mr. Solomon, to be altered. Mr. Solomon asked, "Oh, is your son getting married?" My dad answered that it was his daughter, Arlene. "Do you know a nice Jewish girl for my son?" asked Dad. "As a matter of fact," said Mr. Solomon, "I do." So, Mr. Solomon contacted Joseph Miller and gave me a very good build up. From what Aileen said, she was not so anxious, at first, to be fixed up on a blind date. I was 28 at the time and Aileen was only 19. I believe my age had "reduced" by a few years by Mr. Solomon, the matchmaker.

I talked to Aileen on the phone for the first time just before my sister's wedding for nearly an hour. I have never been much of a talker, so that type of conversation, especially with someone I had never met before, was very unusual. If she was even half as good as she sounded…WOW! I had previously decided to attend the wedding without a date because at the time there was no one I was dating seriously. However, talking to Aileen on the telephone was so comfortable that I was very anxious to meet her and was already considering her to be my wedding date.

When we did meet, Aileen looked even better than she sounded, and things really happened quickly. For one thing, I knew she liked me a lot. To care for someone, and know the feelings are mutual made "liking" turn to "loving" very quickly. If the way to man's heart is through his stomach, Aileen got there in record speed. Aileen invited me to her home and made me delicious dinners. Her mother also would make wonderful meals and had homemade cookies waiting during my visits. Aileen and I both knew within a month that we loved each other and were going to be married.

My parents were on a vacation in Europe when I started dating Aileen. I remember very romantically proposing marriage to her in the Gelson's parking lot in Century City on September 21, 1971. However, we decided to wait until my parents returned from Europe before making the announcement. When I asked Aileen to marry me, she quickly responded with "yes." That to me was much better than "I'll think about it." We both knew that our marriage was right.

When I asked Aileen's father, Joe Miller, for permission to marry his daughter, he smiled, hugged me, and then said, "Good, and you get to pay for the wisdom teeth." I'll never forget that because I thought he was joking. He was not. He sent me the invoice.

Shortly after meeting Aileen, I offered her a job in the offices of Phil Papel Imports. Aileen accepted and helped in typing up invoices. The three remaining office employees from Orange County did not know Aileen and I were dating, so they gossiped about me. Of course, she did not let on. These three women in the office all gave notice at the same time that they were quitting once our relationship became open. This was my first terrible crisis at work, but we hired women from the May Company that were all experienced in the accounts payable office, so the transition went more smoothly than I thought it would. It turned out that Aileen was the only "old-timer" working in the office during our 6-month engagement. So, on March 19, 1972, Aileen Ilona Miller took the hand of Stanley Louis Papel, and a new episode in our lives began.

CHAPTER 5

STANLEY PAPEL
JUST MARRIED (1972–1978)

When we married, Aileen was just 20 and I was 29. Although there was quite an age gap, I did not feel there was a maturity difference in terms of our communication and closeness. I certainly had more experience in terms of college and work than Aileen, but we shared the same values and had other things in common. Additionally, Aileen was very mature for her age while maybe I was still a bit immature. For both of us, it was the beginning of what we hoped to be a lifetime relationship.

We spent our honeymoon in Hawaii visiting Oahu and the big island of Hawaii. It was Aileen's first time in Hawaii, and she was not used to the sun. I kept warning Aileen to avoid getting excessive exposure to the sun, but she was confident she could handle it. Well, she burned and broke out with blisters all over her body. While that dampened portions of the honeymoon, we still had a fabulous time. In a few days she was feeling better, and the honeymoon continued on full force.

After the honeymoon, we resettled in my current apartment. This was probably not a good idea, since Aileen felt like she moved into my place rather than getting a new place that she could decorate to her own liking. This was rectified when we moved upstairs to the largest apartment in the complex, consisting of two bedrooms and a den. The den had a walk-in bar that was a novelty for me at the time.

Another complication arose because the apartment was furnished with my possessions. Aileen felt that there was too much of my identity in our home and not enough room for hers and that I was not inclusive enough of things representing our starting our life together. She told her sister, Dale, the same thing. One day when I came home from work, I discovered that Dale and Aileen had moved all my belongings out of the apartment except for my clothes, stacking them outside in the patio. Of course, an argument took place and, as they say, "the honeymoon was over." After the emotions subsided, I learned a lesson that I have always kept with me. A marriage is a union of two people, and I realized that I had been inconsiderate of Aileen's feelings by dominating our apartment with my possessions. However, although married, we were still individuals, and our individuality needed to be respected as well. I donated or disposed of those items that I did not need or want but saved anything that had a meaning to me. On the negative side, it became apparent that Dale was involved in our married life, and would continue to be involved in issues that should have been between Aileen and me as long as we were married.

One event when we were first married revealed our age difference. Most of my friends were my age and Aileen's friends were her age. One evening, we invited Steve and Nancy Kipper, my accountant and his wife, to dinner. After a lovely dinner prepared by Aileen, we were reminiscing. When Nancy was talking about her high school days in the late 50's, Aileen blurted out, "Oh, I was only in kindergarten then!" The conversation stopped, and Nancy gave Aileen a dagger look that resulted in Aileen never again bringing up her youthfulness to friends in my age bracket. It was hilarious though.

Our marriage brought much happiness into my life. During the first couple of years of our marriage, Aileen and I did many things together. However, we wanted to begin a family before too long into our marriage. I was already in my early thirties, financially ready, and Aileen wanted to be a mother. Although I knew the facts of life by now, I did not realize that it could take more than one or two tries before Aileen became pregnant. Not that trying repeatedly was an unpleasurable experience, but it took about six months before Aileen became pregnant with our first child. Well, all that effort paid off when beautiful Melissa Stephanie Papel was born on February 12, 1974. I had taken Lamaze classes with Aileen; therefore, I was able to share in the birth experience. I will never forget the thrill of being there as Melissa entered the world.

Since Aileen and I had already moved to the upstairs apartment, the baby's room was waiting for her arrival. Melissa was a wonderful baby and brought a new happiness and pride into my life that I did not think was possible. We had a walker, and she would bounce around the apartment in it.

Our family outgrew the apartment very quickly once Melissa arrived. It was time to become homeowners. This was quite a move because we wanted a nice house, but our finances were limited. I had originally wanted to spend $70,000 (this was in 1973), but we ended up spending nearly $100,000 for a lovely but small house in the choice Brentwood neighborhood of Los Angeles at 11837 Kearsarge Street. We did not have to do too much work on the house, but I recall that the previous owners had terrible taste in colors, so we repainted and put new flooring throughout. We stayed in the house only about three years, but it turned out to be a very good investment. We sold the house for more than double what we paid for it.

I was finding that business was challenging and consuming a great deal of my time and energy. The Queen Mary expansion was an immediate success. Even before the permanent 3000 square foot shop opened, we operated kiosks at various locations around the ship. The manager, Boby Williams, had been with my Dad at Ruggles since she was hired in the early days of Disneyland, so all of the operating issues were in good hands. At the peak of our operations aboard the Queen Mary, we had 10 locations and did in the range of $1,000,000 per year in sales.

Ruggles China and Gifts was not quite as lucrative. As a result, we closed a couple of stores and took leases in new malls at Fox Hills in Culver City and the Glendale Galleria. Later we opened more stores, including one in the new Bonaventure Hotel in downtown Los Angeles, and a short-lived fiasco at the Sherman Oaks Galleria.

However, it was the wholesale business, Phil Papel Imports, that caught my interest and energy. The way I looked at it, there were only so many stores that we could open, and each new store brought additional workloads, financial commitments, and constant aggravation. My thinking was that the wholesale business was all under one roof, and if grown wisely it could become very prosperous.

At the time, most of our product line consisted of German lead crystal, English ceramics, and imports from Japan and Taiwan. We served as the primary distributor for larger companies and a few California-made products that were "hot items." My dad always had a knack for identifying a good seller, but the formula did not seem quite right as we had very few products that were unique. I began making trips to the factories Dad worked with, in what was at the time West Germany and in the United Kingdom. I also began going to Asia, but being insecure traveling alone, I would take the inexpensive group tours and then leave the tour group to do my own work in Japan, Taiwan, and Hong Kong.

Aileen accompanied me on many trips to Europe and Asia and learned that my travels were not exactly fun. I remember how excited she was to visit England, only to sit all day in a hot office located above a kiln in a factory on Stoke-on-Trent listening to me bickering over the price of teacups. From that point on, Aileen expressed that she would join me for pleasurable trips such as vacations but declined any more business trips.

We did take a trip to Asia when Melissa was six months old. Later, our parents volunteered to take Melissa for one week. I think she must have been a handful, especially at night because the four grandparents looked a little worn-out after we got back. They were not too quick to offer long-term care again but emphasized that they would take care of her during the days.

Back in California, it seemed that even on my days off, my mind would be on business. Something unspoken began evolving between Aileen and me because of all the time and energy I was devoting to the company. She seemed to resent the time I spent away from the family even though obviously it was what supported our comfortable lifestyle.

It seems that domestic life is very different today than what it was back then. The dynamics which developed had a very negative long-term effect on our marriage, my role as a husband, and even more importantly, as a father. Aileen did not work outside the home once she became a mom and that her time and energy would be best dedicated to being a housewife and mother. My energy was primarily spent earning income for the family so that we could live well. In other words, Aileen was the primary parent in our children's upbringing, and I was the family breadwinner.

The year 1976 was a very special year, even more so than the United States' Bicentennial. Of course, I am alluding to the birth of my son Evan Todd Papel on September 23, 1976. I had really hoped for a son, already having a beautiful daughter. My wish came true when Evan was born. Unlike Melissa, Evan was conceived very quickly, the first month that Aileen did not take precaution. Well, if the conception was easy, that is where it stopped. Evan's birth was anything but easy.

When Aileen and I got to the hospital, Evan decided to stay a while longer before making his grand appearance. Aileen could just not dilate enough, so the doctor finally asked Aileen to get dressed and do some walking. I will never forget running up and down the steps of the Neuropsychiatric Building at Cedars-Sinai Medical Center. I am sure anyone who saw us thought we were escapees! Then Aileen checked back into the hospital when we thought Evan was shaken loose enough, but he was still not ready. The doctor said he would not ask Aileen to leave again, and I am sure what he was doing was inducing labor. Even though we had taken the Lamaze refresher and I was initially allowed in the labor room, it became apparent that Evan was not coming easily, so the doctor told me to leave. This made me very nervous. When Evan was finally born, he was all purple—and I was a wreck. Evan eventually lightened up and I was told he was just fine. Melissa was hard to conceive, but she slipped out easily. Evan's birth aged me quickly.

Evan was a serious baby and did not smile much at first. Aileen used to hold him and laugh to get Evan to giggle back. I think it worked, and I credit Aileen in the initial development of Evan's happy personality. He developed childhood asthma at the Kearsarge house, so we installed linoleum in his room replacing the hazardous carpet. I recall that every time the weather changed, there would be a big bubble in the center of his floor because the linoleum had been installed improperly. For Melissa's room I bought a big cardboard playhouse. Sometimes I played inside the house with Melissa, although it was a tight fit for me.

During this time we got our first dog, a dachshund named Gretchen. I had loved my parents' dachshund, Ginger, so I hoped our new puppy would be as lovable. Unfortunately, Gretchen was a very nervous dog, and she would pee every time she was tense. Of course, Aileen got tired of wiping up pee, especially on our new carpeting. Once, we hosted an entourage of Japanese visitors from the Hayashi mug factory. Mr. Hayashi went to pet Gretchen and she turned over on her back, spread her legs, and made a fountain of pee over him. That was the last straw, and we ended up finding a good home for Gretchen with a woman who had another dachshund.

One evening while we still had Gretchen, I heard a sound in the kitchen. I thought it was Gretchen, but figured I better investigate. In the dark, I saw movement of what I thought was Gretchen. I turned on the light and to my astonishment, it was a huge rat! I was so startled that I screamed and jumped onto whatever was nearby. We had ivy in our backyard attracting rats, and it must have come through the doggie door.

Every time I went overseas, there would always be many aggravating problems at the house When I came home and after the reunion with Aileen and the kids, I would check the bills to see what disaster had happened during my last trip. One time, I saw a bill from "The Fish Doctor" for $42. I was curious what that could be. Aileen swallowed hard and said she accidentally turned up the thermostat on my aquarium and "boiled the fish." Her dad was out of town, and she could not get anyone to come over to scoop out all the dead fish. Therefore, she had to call "The Fish Doctor" to perform a burial service in our toilet.

In 1974, Phil Papel Imports began decorating mugs. What began as a special name mug program for the Queen Mary stores turned into a general personalized name program. By 1975, sales of personalized name mugs really exploded. The company was selling mugs as quickly as it could decorate them. Sales went from $700,000 the year before to nearly $3,000,000 within one year. The kiln operated 24 hours a day in three shifts, and we needed to rent additional locations to store and ship the mugs to nearby warehouses. At one point, Papel Imports had four warehouses on Mettler and Crocker Street in an increasingly dangerous neighborhood. This necessitated all types of security measures, and even at that, there were robberies and other dangers at nearby businesses. Once, a representative of our retail stores while calling at the warehouse was attacked and dragged down the street because she would not release her handbag to the robbers who had attacked her.

Both wholesale and retail businesses were very profitable for us in the late 70's. However, within a couple of years, the high rate of sales on the name mugs declined due to competition and the life cycle of the product. Fortunately, the personalized mugs sales were replaced with other strong mug series such as "World's Greatest…" mugs and "Kiss Me… I'm Jewish, Bald, Horny, etc." mugs. It is hard to believe that no one before Papel Imports thought of mugs as a form of social and personal expression. In 1975 and 1976, we had virtually 100 percent of this market. Soon other companies saw that Papel was on to something very lucrative. While losing market share over time, Papel Imports maintained itself as the market leader for mugs throughout the late 70's and into the 80's.

By 1978, it was obvious the company could no longer continue to operate out of four warehouses in southeast Los Angeles. We began to search therefore for a large central warehouse and offices in a safer neighborhood. My dad was in charge of the search and negotiations; however, everything that looked attractive was out of reach financially, and for a while, it appeared that only relocation to Valencia or Newberry Park would be affordable. Both of these areas are on the far fringes of Los Angeles County, and it meant any employee would have to relocate their home. However, we became lucky, when someone who had refused to sell to us before changed his mind because of health reasons. So, my dad finalized the purchase of a 70,000 square foot warehouse, later expanded to 100,000 square feet, at 7355 Lankershim Boulevard in North Hollywood.

At the same time, Aileen and I began looking for a larger house. Kearsarge Street had become too small for us, and a larger house was something we felt could not wait for much longer. During our search, we considered a fixer-upper in Beverly Hills that turns out would have made us a fortune the way real estate price escalated in the next few years. However, we found a new house that proved to be irresistible. I remember Aileen phoning me to drop everything to come see this great house. Aileen was right, and we were able to negotiate a very good price of roughly $238,000 for 17140 Weddington Street in Encino. We told the builder to stop the remaining work, primarily carpets, curtains, and finishing touches, so we could choose what we liked and to keep the final price to a minimum. At the end of 1978, we moved to our new home and relocated the business. A new chapter in our lives was about to begin.

CHAPTER 6

STANLEY PAPEL
THE UP AND DOWN YEARS (1978–1990)

The years from 1978 through 1990 reflect a unique new chapter in my life, beginning with my family's move from Brentwood to Encino, California, and ending with my leaving Papel Giftware. This period symbolizes for me happy and sad times, gains and losses, and many right and wrong directions. When I look back at these years, they seem like a blend of mixed emotions, and they set the stage for my first midlife crisis.

Often, I reflect on these years with regret. This was the time when business and personal life seemed more and more to conflict. I wanted to have the business succeed to provide security for my family and myself. However, as the years progressed, I became more acutely aware that the time and energy I devoted to the business was alienating me from my family. When I would come home from business trips, I was reminded of missing many family events, especially those related to Melissa's and Evan's schooling. Also, there were frequently things going wrong with the house, so I felt guilty that Aileen had to handle everything involving home and family life while I was away on business. At the same time, I felt personal satisfaction from succeeding in business and in being able to grow the business to provide not only for the financial security of my family but also for the many devoted employees that worked at Papel.

In 1981 my cousin Geri Roth Jacobson had a retinal detachment. Because I had seen a couple of dark spots, I thought I should have my eyes checked just in case this problem could run in the family. I went to an ophthalmologist who dilated my eyes and started the examination. As the examination progressed, it became very apparent from the length of the examination and his lack of communication that something was wrong. Finally, he told me I have very serious degenerate lattice, which is a retinal problem. He said both eyes' retinas were ready to detach at any moment and that I was a "time bomb waiting to explode." Even a tennis ball hitting me in the head would be enough to detach a retina. I was in shock, could not see from the dilation, and just could not believe what I was hearing. I remember phoning Aileen and then waiting until my eyes cleared up enough, so that I could drive home. The next day, we saw two more doctors who confirmed the same diagnosis but had a better bedside manners. I decided that I wanted Dr. Gerald Sanders to perform the surgeries because he seemed the most conservative and I had confidence in him. He wanted to perform four separate surgeries: upper left, upper right, lower left, and lower right. Dr. Sanders felt that there would be too much trauma to the eyes to complete the procedure in one or two surgeries. Over a period of nearly a year going into 1982, the surgeries were performed using cryotherapy, which is a freezing technique. It was fortunate that there were four separate surgeries as Dr. Sanders had recommended, as there were complications on the third with hemorrhaging. If the entire eye had been operated on at once, there would have been more serious complications.

I handled the surgeries well. I admit I was petrified especially going into the first surgery. However, I knew I was strong and determined enough to get through this crisis. Aileen was my Nurse Nightingale during this whole time. It was very difficult on her, but she was always there for me and nursed some gory-looking eyes.

The business helped keep my mind off my problems. I was on the phone constantly during recuperation and having meetings at my house. I was also mistakenly indebted to the new president I had hired just days before finding about the eye problem. I felt it was a miracle that I had hired someone who would oversee the administrative issues just as I was no longer able to do so. When I finally recovered, my eyes were repaired to a point that I would not have to be concerned about retinal detachments. There were some after-effects—"floaters" or black areas in my vision -that I have learned to cope with, and over time my optical cones and rods were affected so that I currently do not adapt well to seeing at night. Even so, the world seemed much more beautiful with my new-found appreciation of my vision. I made a promise to myself to improve my physical condition from that point onward. I have to say that I have kept up on this promise to myself. After the surgeries, I said I would take time to appreciate the beauty of life. Unfortunately, I did not fulfill this personal promise until several years later. In 1982, I was only 40 years old but certainly initiated into one midlife crisis.

These were also formative years for Melissa and Evan, and as I look back, I wish I had been home for them more. Melissa was affected the most when I missed her birthdays which always coincided with the Birmingham Fair tradeshow in England. Although we would celebrate right before I left or after I got back, this hurt her as I learned later.

We did have some good times as a family during those years. One of the highlights was our trip to Israel for three weeks in 1987. We had a wonderful guide who took us to not only the typical tourist sights but also several off-the-beaten-path places.

We also went to San Diego or other local areas each summer with our closest friends, Bernie and Sue Kamins and their daughters, Marni and Piper. And I used to take the kids separately to breakfast once in a while.

Aileen and I took some wonderful trips together without the children, including to the United Kingdom, Netherlands, Russia, Finland, the Orient, Mexico, Hawaii, Montreal, Argentina, Australia, and New Zealand. Probably our favorite was the week we spent together in New Zealand because of the beauty of the Southern Island and the friendliness of the people in the Northern Island. In retrospect, though, I think it was a time that Aileen and I could focus on being with each other and could reconnect as husband and wife without the pressures of family and business we experienced daily.

However, our differences seemed to be growing. Aileen had been seeing a therapist for many years, and we began marriage counseling together. Ostensibly, the therapy was in recognition of the fact that our marriage had been "status quo" for a number of years and that we wanted to be closer. The therapist said that in her experience marriages do not stay the same. Over time, spouses either grow closer together or further apart. Having two beautiful children and remembering some very happy times earlier in our marriage, I truly hoped that Aileen and I would get closer. I also began seeing a therapist, Mike Silverman, as I was feeling very inadequate as a father and husband and was coming to terms with some personal issues. My life was stressful, I felt overworked, and I knew that Aileen was unhappy with me and our marriage. Although I was successful in business, I felt that other important parts of my life were failures.

Now as I look back, am I sorry that so much of my energy was devoted to business during this period? Yes and No. I would never intentionally have hurt the people I loved by directing so much of myself to business. However, I believed then that the time I spent on business was primarily to provide security for myself and my family. While we were not rolling in money, my wife and children did not ever worry about having the material things that they desired. My son Evan told me later that the family would have preferred fewer material things and more of me. While at this point, I agree that time spent with him and the rest of my family would have been better, I do hope that maybe someday he will understand why I did what I did. I had only the example of my own father. I did not understand or appreciate until many years later the value of interpersonal closeness and family time.

After I sold the business in 1987 and was "out" of Papel Giftware, there was a lot of mental adjustment to take place. In some respects, when I sold the business, I felt like I was selling a child. The business was handed down to me by my father; I had hoped someday my children would be involved in the business as well. This would no longer be possible. In addition, there were so many long-term dedicated employees and sales representatives who had been with Papel for many years. Was I selling them out? What would their future be after the transition of new ownership took over?

Then I would think that the business was not really like a person at all. It was just a vehicle for making a livelihood. It had drained so much from me, and selling the company would give me a chance to enjoy life more as well as provide financial security for my family. While I look back at this time as being one long crisis, there were some very happy times.

One highlight of this time and one of the happiest events in my lifetime was the birth of my youngest daughter, Dara Michelle Papel, on August 1, 1986. There is a very humorous story around the conception of Dara. Aileen was on a trip to Asia with me in early 1986. This was Aileen's second trip to Asia, the first being back in 1974 when Melissa was just six months old. During the first trip, Aileen had visited Hayashi's mug factory, our supplier of personalized name mugs.

During the second trip in 1986, I told Aileen that we were going back to the Hayashi mug factory. Instead, I surprised her and we visited the Penis Shrine. There were penis shrubs; stones carved in shapes of penises; even a lady selling penis-shaped cookies. There was also a 10-foot penis woodcarving. Aileen was expecting to see mugs and was flabbergasted by the symbol of the shrine. Of course, she touched the 10-foot penis. Later, we were told the Penis Shrine is for fertility and that people visit it to pray to become pregnant. Aileen was told then that touching the penis carving increases the chance of pregnancy. Therefore, when we returned the United

States and Aileen discovered that she was pregnant, it turned out to be correct. We often joke that Dara was born with a label on her bottom, "Made in Japan."

When Aileen was pregnant with Dara, we decided to add onto the house and built two bedrooms and a den upstairs. Previously we had built a room in the garage for the dozen-plus housekeepers over the years. Now the housekeeper, Conche, would get Evan's old room, and Melissa's room would be converted into the baby's room. The add-on took a few months and for quite a while, when it did not have a roof, Melissa and Evan camped in our bedroom. Getting the house finished was nip and tuck with the time Dara was scheduled to arrive. I think the paint was still wet in Dara's room when she was born.

Dara, 10 and 12 years younger than Evan and Melissa, made her entry into the world a family affair. Even choosing Dara's name was something we were all involved in. At first, we could not think of a good name to choose for a girl. Then, the family was at Knott's Berry Farm watching a performance where a beautiful girl, Darrah, was being hypnotized. We had never heard that name before, and we all looked at each other and at once knew that would be her name.

Dara's birth was not easy for Aileen. I had taken a Lamaze refresher and felt like the grandpa in the group, especially when we took the hospital tour. I was already 43 years old and most of the fathers-to-be were in their twenties.

Dara was born with clubbed feet and a condition which we had never heard of called arthrogryposis, a congenital curvature of the joints with muscle shortening and weakness, such that the flexing of the affected areas was impossible or painful. Although we were told Dara's case was mild, it was difficult as parents to see what our child was going through. Although Dara would not remember this, from the very first day of her life she was in casts. At the beginning, Aileen and Conche moved her casts twice each week. Then she would be taken to Dr. Bernstein's office where new casts would be placed on her legs and feet. At six months old, Dara had her first of three surgeries. In this surgery, they corrected her club feet and did additional reconstructive surgery on both feet.

We did not raise Dara any differently than Melissa or Evan because of arthrogryposis. I think that the love Dara received from the entire family resulted in her being a happy child. Dara did not know that what she was experiencing in those days was any different from other infants. However, as parents, we felt all the pain that Dara endured. I will never forget the helplessness of my seeing my six-month old child coming out of surgery still anesthetized and pure white.

Aileen had become somewhat active in communicating with other parents of children with arthrogryposis. There was no active national organization, but we did make a trip to Chicago where there was a small group attempting to put together a national organization.

Melissa was 12 years old when Dara was born and in the process of preparing for her Bat Mitzvah. One of the additional events that made the occasion even more special was that we wanted to name Dara at the Bat Mitzvah service. The Rabbi said this was the first time that the temple had a baby naming and Bat Mitzvah of two sisters at the same service. The Bat Mitzvah was a beautiful occasion, although I vaguely remember that it seemed that everything that could have gone wrong did so in terms of all the preparations Aileen had made. I remember that, at first, we could not find the note cards for Melissa's candle lighting service, but Melissa was so cool about everything and really handled everything with much poise.

That period was also the time we were having financial difficulties at the business. I was not taking a salary that year and was very concerned that our personal assets could be attached by the bank. I had already loaned the company over $300,000, and I was becoming drained both financially and mentally. To some extent, this also affected how lavishly we could spend on the Bat Mitzvah although I do not think anyone noticed where we had to cut down on the spending.

Nevertheless, in June 1987, we did take a very special family two-week trip (except for Dara) to Israel. I had accumulated more than enough frequent traveler miles on Pan Am Airlines for four free first-class tickets to Israel. We economized on the hotel accommodations, but our treat was a private tour guide for several of those days. He was a retired army officer who knew the country well and who kept us very busy. Once the trip was over, I knew I had some very big decisions to make about the business.

I was unaware of the extent of conversations that the previous president had held with a major giftware company, Applause, about the possibility of our being acquired. They contacted me in 1987 asking me if I was still interested. I told them I was interested in listening to them. Before long, it was apparent that they were going to make a proposal to acquire Papel. At that point, I contacted a business broker, Jim Freedman, to handle the negotiations. He did a spectacular job in getting other companies interested in buying Papel as well. Soon there was a bidding war between Applause and Russ Berrie and Company with Russ Berrie coming through with a cash offer to buy the company, repay the debt to my parents and me, and to continue my employment under contract through 1990.

I had extreme reservations about selling the company. All types of reasons went through my head as to why I should or should not sell. I asked my dad how he would feel if I sold the company. He said he just wanted me to have happiness and peace of mind. He said it was definitely all right with him if I sold it. So, in August 1987, the company Papel Giftware was sold to Russ Berrie and Company, and I had to adjust to being an employee for at least the next three years.

According to what I was told, more often than not when a business is sold it is difficult for the previous owner to work happily in the new environment. I was determined to defy the odds and continue working at Papel, hopefully on a long-term basis. I was only 44 when I sold the company; however, my hopes in this respect did not materialize.

There was a honeymoon phase at the beginning when everything went very smoothly. When our overseas purchases merged into the Russ Berrie offices, I observed some matters that I thought were not in the best interest of the corporation. Being outspoken on the matters, I stepped on the wrong toes. While I continued to put my best efforts into the company, I realized I did not fit into the new corporate structure. I think I had been an entrepreneur too long to change in a way that would fit the mode under the new structure.

As I look back, 1988-1990 was a very sad time in my career. I saw the disintegration of what formerly had been Papel and the transformation of the company into the image of the parent company. In May 1990, I was asked to leave the company, although my contract did not expire until December 1990. I did not leave right away but completed some projects that I was working on and finally left in July. It was a sad ending for me after 20 years of hard work at Papel. Yet, as I look back, I am not sorry at all that I sold Papel, given the stress it was causing me. And its sale assured that my family and I could have financial security in the future.

CHAPTER 7

STANLEY PAPEL

CHANGES ARE COMING (1990–1995)

My father-in-law, Joseph Miller, had been battling leukemia for years. It was not apparent at first, but by 1989 things took a turn for the worse. He began deteriorating much more rapidly. This was around the time that Evan's Bar Mitzvah was approaching. It was a bittersweet time, especially for Aileen. Many of her Canadian relatives were planning to come to the Bar Mitzvah, and I believe my father-in-law willed himself to live for Evan's Bar Mitzvah. Although he could not attend the ceremony or party, he was able to hear about it from his hospital room. Although we were sorry that my father-in-law could not attend, it did not change the happiness of the event and how proud we were of Evan. Two weeks after the Bar Mitzvah, Joe Miller passed away. Our family was profoundly moved and very sad to see him pass.

After Joe Miller passed away, my brother-in-law Barry Siegel and I worked on cleaning up his estate. It was a very sad situation because he had amassed considerable business and personal debts. This made it all the more difficult for my mother-in-law, Adele Miller. Joe had purchased a life insurance policy that was worthless. It made me realize how important it was to be financially responsible and accumulate savings. I decided then to have a family trust where there would be sound financial safeguards for my family and loved ones. At the same time, I gained tremendous respect for my brother-in-law. He was going through a divorce, but still did everything within his power to make the things go as smoothly as possible for the family.

I bought a condominium near us for Adele to move into. Following her father's death, Aileen went into a deep depression, and I tried to be there for her during this time. It took about 14 months for Aileen to be herself again. My mother-in-law was also very sad, but something good happened after she moved into the condominium. Across the way, there was a man by the name of Al Ganz, who fell madly in love with Adele. He courted her and treated her like a princess. I had a fondness for Al, especially when he very cutely asked for *my* permission to marry my mother-in-law. I will never forget that. It was such a role reversal. Of course, I gave him my permission, stating that I am not losing a mother-in-law, but rather I am gaining a father-in-law.

After leaving Papel Giftware in 1990, I became a student again, this time at California State University at Northridge. I enrolled in several classes that I had always wanted to take, while deciding what I wanted to do next. I leased a small office on Ventura Boulevard near my home and began putting files together on new products to be developed for the giftware market. I considered where I might go in the future, but I knew I was not ready to retire. I also recognized that I wanted to remain in the giftware industry since I was established and had been comfortable in it for the last 20 years. However, I did not want to start another company that just imported and warehoused products. I thought the best business venture for me would be developing new giftware products to license to other importers and manufacturers. Moreover, this start-up would not conflict with the non-competition clause that was in effect through the end of 1991. Eventually, the corporation that I still owned, Ruggles Gifts, became S. Papel & Company, later renamed Papel Designs.

By 1991, I had hired a part-time assistant in Product Development, and the new small company was operative. My account base grew quite rapidly, and I quickly had projects that I could handle with my very small staff. It was a strange feeling to be "on my own" with the real sense of not having a large back-up support staff as I had at Papel for so many years. In starting the new company, I made a very conscious decision that I did not want the company to grow larger even if the opportunity developed over time. By the end of 1991, I had two major accounts in the USA, Otagiri and Ganz as well as accounts with importers in Europe and Australia, and had signed up manufacturers that wished to license designs directly from me. In 1992 my sister Arlene joined me briefly, working directly for Ganz. However, within a few months it was apparent that an additional office was needed just to handle the Ganz account. Arlene was in charge of Product Development for Ganz, and I concentrated on the other accounts that we had previously worked with.

At the same time, there were a couple of other troubling areas related to business. I had been in litigation with Russ Berrie and Company for nearly a year over the use of my family name in the giftware industry. When I sold Papel, Inc., I sold the trade name and trademark "Papel" but never gave up the right for me to use my own name as an individual in the industry. However, when products were later introduced into the marketplace containing my copyright notice, Russ Berrie and Company contended that it caused confusion. I tried to settle the dispute by agreeing to use my name in small type as copyright notice in conjunction with the company that had licensed the design. While that was not acceptable to them at the beginning, several months later the dispute was settled, assuring me the right to use my name as an individual as I had originally proposed. Psychologically, it was important for me to use my name if I so choose.

The other battle going on concurrently was at the Papel warehouse. Originally it had been leased by Russ Berrie and Company, the new owners of Papel. After a period of time, they vacated the building although my parents and I had retained ownership of it The rent revenues from this building had been a major source of our income, so a vacancy here during a severe recession in California was very troubling. For several months, brokers had attempted to lease the building without success. Property prices and leasing rates continued to tumble and the idea of the building remaining vacant for an extended period became a reality. During these troubled times, there were riots in South Central Los Angeles with portions of the city being devastated by fires. Consequently, some buildings where swap meets had been held were burned down leaving the swap meets searching for alternate locations. Our building was located in a residential area, and it was large enough and well suited to be converted to a "swap meet mini mall." The benefit was that we would receive rentals based upon retail rental rates, which were significantly higher than warehouse rental rates. So, a new lease was finalized to have the warehouse space converted into more than 100 stalls as a swap meet mall at a rental figure significantly higher than what Papel had paid. However, "high risk–high reward" had its drawbacks and several bounced checks later, the original masters' tenants were evicted after a court battle. A new lease was later signed with the current tenants. Although there are ongoing problems with the building and the tenant, we receive our rent checks on time.

CHAPTER 8

STANLEY PAPEL
COMING OUT STORY (1995)

In 1995 when I got back from Nepal, I decided to write myself a message. I sent it to a few close friends because I wanted to share my feelings. Also, I wanted what I said to be a public commitment, not just words on paper:

April 17, 1995

Before I get too caught up in the return to normalcy of life in the USA, I think it would be good for me to reflect on few thoughts from Nepal.

The combination of the physical and mental tasks I experienced during the last two weeks had a profound effect on my attitudes about many things in life. The trip has stimulated me to begin writing my life story, to be given to my children at a later date. In the process many memories and feelings that have been tucked away for years have surfaced to my consciousness.

I saw a way of life in Nepal that I could not have seen any other way but to go on foot through the Himalayas. We took a route which passed through many remote areas. Many other trekkers were unable to traverse this route because of the restricted permits to the area. I saw a way of life which had very few of the comforts we enjoy, yet the people seemed very content and happy in their lives.

To put this in perspective, the people I met direct much of their energy into what will bring them happiness in their lives, while we seem to direct most of our energy into things that do not bring us happiness. The contrast between their focus and that of myself and everyone I knew was striking. I could not help but wonder if they may be better off than the Americans or other wealthier Westerners that have more material possessions.

We have the stress and pressures of a modern society. In Nepal, I perceived that the villagers were happier and less stressed than we are. I know that many of the other trekkers were affected by this realization just as I was.

Many of the things I thought were important in my life are not really so important. Many of the things that I have pushed to the side have become important. I am definitely at a stage in my life now that I can reduce the amount of energy that I direct towards business. As a result, I can use some of this energy toward family, friends and self.

I should put more of my time into fulfilling aspects of life that will enhance me mentally and physically. I should spend more time with those that I love and show them that I care. I know from experience that it is easier to write things down than actually do them. However, I will make a very strong effort to turn these words into reality.

When I began to write this life story back in 1995, there were some things bothering me very much. I could not say everything I wanted to say. I had secrets. I thought, "Should I keep these secrets to myself all my life, or should I become more open and honest with myself and others, especially in this book?" There were parts of my life that I was very unhappy about. The Nepal trip brought them to the surface. I was not happily married and had not been for a number of years. I wondered, "Should I continue to work with Aileen to try to improve our relationship, or is it time to make a major change in my life?" I wished to lead a traditional married life, while I kept what I considered deep dark secrets about another part of my being.

The fact is that I am gay. It was in the month of May 1995 that I came out at the age of 52. However, to tell you my coming out story I must digress back to the summer of 1969 when I was 26 years old.

I was staying near Greenwich Village at the time. I remember reading about the police raid at the Stonewall Inn on the fateful Saturday of June 28, 1969. The Stonewall Inn was a bar frequented by gays. They gathered there because there were few other venues to share that part of their identity. At the time, bars in New York were run by the Mob. It was known that the Mafia paid protection money to the police so that the police would not interfere with what went on in the bars. Evidently, the Mafia was behind in payments, so the police raided Stonewall. The gays, especially the drag queens, put up a fight against the police that escalated into a riot, opening eyes and raising spirits, and marking the beginning of the gay rights movement.

Back in the 1960's, there had been anti-war demonstrations, student activism, woman's liberation, and a movement towards liberalism. However, being homosexual then was illegal, a psychiatric perversion, and a Biblical abomination. During that time young and old men lived lives of silent angst, in desperate fear of being found out, humiliated, fired from jobs, beaten, or even murdered. Thus, many homosexual men were in the closet. They were forced to live a traditional lifestyle and keep their sexuality a secret. I was one of those men.

At 26 years old, I was aware of my attraction to men. However, being a "nice Jewish boy," what I wanted in my life was to be married, have children, be successful in business, and have a stable and happy life. At that time being gay was associated with men who were feminine, flighty, and unstable. I did not want any of that for my life. I decided that my gay desires would remain my secret, and that I would lead a traditional life. After all, homosexuality was considered a mental illness, and I did not want that as part of my profile. I was dating many women at the time and considered a good catch. I was even attracted to women; I was just more attracted to men. I had graduated with my MBA two years earlier. I had a successful job with May Department Stores. At the time I was looking for a woman to share my life with. Stonewall was just something that happened, and nothing that affected me personally. I did not realize that it would spark a movement which would eventually lead to the achievement of gay rights

Today in California it is not illegal to be gay, and it is no longer considered to be a mental disorder. There are equal rights in the workplace. While there are still strong feelings against gays by many of the USA population, the homophobia does not compare to what it was back in the 1960's. Coming out today is not anything like coming out in 1969.

So fast forward from 1969: I married in 1972 and started a family with Aileen in 1974. For most of the subsequent 23 years I remained married, sometimes happily, sometimes unhappily, while keeping my secret. Aileen and I ended up going to marriage counselors for years. However, our efforts to become closer were of no avail.

Sometime in 1993 I discovered the gay sites on the Internet. Again, those sites were very different from what is available today. I joined an Internet website called Delos which had online bulletin boards where men posted messages that could be read only by others who were registered at the same site. Back then one could venture to send private messages to unknown people via the bulletin boards, which were the start of emailing. At the website I joined a group called "Gay Married Men" where I learned there were many other men who shared my circumstances. I discovered that there were many married men, some with children who had gay feelings. Many were in love and still happy with their wives. Many others were frustrated and sad. It was an eye-opener for me to realize that I was not alone in life. In fact, it was estimated then that there were over 2 million married gay men and over 1 million gay fathers. At that time, gay fathers had children the natural biological way with women, artificial insemination had not been introduced, and gay men were not allowed to adopt children.

The story of how I came out is not a good one. It is difficult for me to write about because it involved hurting others. To give you the background, I need to reiterate a few things that were happening in my life. As I started my life story in 1995 after the Nepal trip, I reflected on my life and realized that I had come to a point where I was living my life as a lie, and I could not continue living this way.

In May 1995, Aileen and I decided to seek therapy again about our marriage. Aileen was going to have a hysterectomy that month, so we were going to wait until she was over the worst of the surgery. We had gone in the past to both Aileen's psychologist and my psychologist; this time we were going to my psychologist. He had already asked me, "Do you think that the outcome will be any different this time than the last time?" I said, "No, but I must stay married until Dara is past the critical growing up years." I had discussed with him that I wanted to separate from Aileen after Dara's Bat Mitzvah, which was still 4 1/2 years away. My psychologist suggested, however, that perhaps Aileen and I should discuss an immediate separation during our next round of counseling sessions.

Third, I was very involved in the gay sites on the Internet; finding out about and communicating with other married gay men had been an eye-opener for me. I was beginning to feel more and more that there was not anything wrong with me. The effects of Stonewall were reaching me 25 years later. I certainly was not ready to come out in May 1995, but I no longer felt the shame and aloneness that had been with me for much of my life.

Then, on an evening in late May, concurrent with the time Aileen was having her hysterectomy, I received a phone call from my daughter, Melissa. She was attending the University of Arizona at the time. I answered the phone to receive these words, which I will never forget, "You need to talk to Evan about your e-mails." She did not need to state anything more. Although I saved no messages on the computer, I realized at that moment, both my daughter and son knew that I was exchanging gay-related messages on the Internet. My heart dropped. I could hardly speak. It turned out that Evan had accessed my computer because he was curious as to what I was spending so much time on. And he knew, with his technical savvy, that he would be able to read my personal emails.

I said to Melissa, "I have been exchanging messages with gay married men," but I did not admit that I was one of them. The next day I called Melissa back and came out to her. She told me that Evan had indeed accessed my e-mails, and the following day I came out to Evan. I told both Melissa and Evan that I had decided to separate from their mother. However, I wanted to wait until after she recovered from her surgery and was in a better physical condition to handle the disclosure. Both Melissa and Evan agreed to keep the secret for about a month during Aileen's recovery. We also decided to go to Catalina for a few days and just talk through what was happening with our lives.

At that moment in time, Melissa seemed to be handling everything quite well, although any life change like this can affect us deeply. But Evan was angry with me about the "deception" issue, meaning my deception of him and the entire family. While he had invaded my privacy on the computer, that breach was minimal compared to the issues of coming out to my family and making the decision to separate from Aileen.

It was in early July 1995 that I came out to Aileen; both Melissa and Evan were present. Aileen said she had felt that there was a problem but did not know what it was. She said she didn't have any idea that I was attracted to men, so the whole thing was a shock to her. She offered to work with me on it, but I told her that there were many issues and that I felt that I needed to separate. Aileen asked me if I had any intent to have sexual contact with men, and I replied, "yes." She reminded me that I had taken a vow to fidelity, so if I were going to have any sex outside of marriage, whether with a man or a woman, she would want a divorce. I said I could respect her decision, and that we would end up divorced anyway. I suggested that we go towards this goal as amicably as possible.

Dara was away at "sleep-away camp." We feared that if she came home and found us in process of divorce, then it would be even more traumatic for her than just the realization that her father was gay. She would be afraid to ever leave home again for fear of something terrible happening while she was away. So I decided it was important to delay the divorce until a later time when it would be easier for Dara to understand. Dara was coming home from sleep-away camp towards the end of July 1995. Then, it was her 9th birthday on August 1, 1995, so I would technically stay in the house until after her birthday.

The first night after I came out to Aileen, we actually slept in the same bed. The following night, however, Aileen said it would be better if I slept in Dara's bed. Two days later, Aileen said it would be for the best if I moved out. I immediately moved out of my 5,400 square foot home, taking only my clothes, and into an 800 square foot apartment in Canoga Park. Later, I had my desk and a few personal possessions moved. The day before Dara came back from camp, I moved temporarily back to the house at Weddington Street.

The time between Dara arriving back home and her birthday party was a very difficult time for all of us. A few days after Dara's birthday, Aileen, I, Melissa and Evan were all present as I came out to Dara. The coming-out issue by itself was not upsetting to Dara; it was the breakup of the family because of the ensuing divorce that concerned her. She was just listening, and then she said, "Does that mean you are going to divorce?" Aileen and I both said, "yes." I will never forget the distressed expression on Dara's face. I tried to remember what my psychologist had told me. "When two parents live together and are unhappy, it isn't a good thing for the children. They can be better off with two parents that are happy and do not live together. Dara will know that she is loved by both parents." I kept thinking, "Please let this be true. Please let this be true."

I then came out to my mother at her condo. My dad had already been diagnosed with Alzheimer's and was at the stage that he could not understand daily events. I started by telling my mom that Aileen and I were having marital problems and that we had decided to divorce. I also told her that I was attracted to men and that I was gay. I was previously unable to say those words. My mom said that she hadn't ever thought of me as gay, but it did not change anything about the way she felt about me and that she loved me. She got up from her chair, walked over, and gave me a big hug as we both cried. She did warn me, "Just be careful. If anything ever happens to you, it would kill me." I reassured her that I would be careful; AIDS was in everyone's mind, and I knew how important it was to be safe. At that stage, I had not had much experience with men.

I then came out to other people that I was close to. I told my cousin, Rochelle Papel. She said, "I always knew you were gay. I love you and just be happy." My best friend Bernie Kamins said, "I knew you were gay. I didn't know if YOU knew you were gay. I figured if you wanted to tell me, you would." Again, I was surprised and pleased at the total acceptance of me coming out. All of my cousins were supportive as were most of my friends, with the exception of some married couples that Aileen and I had been friendly with. Overall, I think that the main issue was the divorce rather than my sexual orientation, which resulted not keeping in touch with some of them.

When I told my sister Arlene, however, she said that she was shocked and knew nothing about these things. Nevertheless, she said that she still loved me, but she felt that she did not know me. It was not exactly what I wanted to hear as I would have liked stronger support and understanding. At the same time, I knew that she still loved me.

I am no longer ashamed of being gay. I have no regrets that I married Aileen, as I believe we both fully loved each other at the time. At the beginning of our marriage, it was very healthy and happy. I know it was a mistake for both Aileen and I to stay married for so long. We were like "oil" and "water," neither bad, but not mixing well. We should have separated and divorced before Dara was born. However, if we had not stayed married, then Dara would not be here today. How can I be sorry about my married life? Aileen and I brought three beautiful children into this world.

Stanley Papel. First Gay Cruise in 1996

CHAPTER 9

STANLEY PAPEL
THE TRANSITION YEARS (1995–1998)

During the next three years I transitioned from a traditional lifestyle to being comfortable as a gay man. I was in my early 50's and had some "growing up" to do, which is typical for men who have kept such an important part of themselves concealed. It was also a very reflective time for me as I thought a lot about my past, present, and future. Those years were like a second childhood, or perhaps part of the childhood and adulthood that I never permitted myself to experience. They became the foundation of coming to terms with myself and accepting who I am. A saying that I like is "It's never too late to have a happy childhood. The second one is up to you and no one else." Not that my childhood was unhappy, but I felt that starting in 1995, I was taking control of the rest of my life and determined that it would be happy and fulfilling.

I had come to terms with the fact that my marriage had been unhappy for many years. Although I had stayed married, seeming to enjoy a traditional, happy life, deep inside I was very despondent about the lack of communication between Aileen and me. I also felt guilty about my sexual desires. Aileen was continually pointing out my shortcomings. Nearly every day, there was bickering between us. I don't blame Aileen; I blame "us." When I came out, I felt unworthy and had a very low self-esteem, although I still felt confident about my business abilities. I felt guilty for leaving the house and not being there for Dara. I was afraid of the future. What would life be like going forward? Yet there was a sense of relief since I no longer needed to keep secrets. Whatever the future would bring, at least I was being open and honest with myself and with others.

At the time of the separation, which officially occurred July 19, 1995, my business was downsizing in scope. I needed something to fill in my life to take the place of the collapsed marriage and separation from the family, the decreased business activity, and the challenges of a different lifestyle. The apartment complex in Canoga Park where I had moved when Aileen and I separated was frequented by singles and newly divorced or separated people. It was not a home setting that I was accustomed to, downsizing from a luxurious 5400 square foot home in Encino to an 800 square foot, two-bedroom apartment with leased furniture.

Soon after the separation, I set some goals for myself, which I can still clearly recall:

1. To maintain and increase my bond with Dara. While it was also important to have a strong relationship with Melissa and Evan, they were already in college and not as vulnerable as Dara.

2. To remain close with my mom and assist my dad who was battling Alzheimer's disease.

3. To resolve the issues related to the pending divorce so that Aileen and I could move forward with our lives.

4. To find a good home to settle in the Los Angeles area (preferably in the city instead of the San Fernando Valley).

5. To increase my business results

6. To learn more about the gay community and get any necessary therapy.

7. To find a passion.

8. To make new friends and keep old friends.

9. To meet someone whom I could share the rest of my life with.

The most special times during this era of my life were with my mom and with Dara, with whom I spent every other weekend. Dara and I took many trips together. I had a timeshare in San Francisco at the Donatello. For many years we would go there for three or four days at a time. Other special trips during this time immediately following my separation from Aileen were to Washington D.C. in 1997, Orlando, Florida, to Disney World and Epcot, and a family vacation in 1998 to Hawaii with my mom, Melissa, and Dara.

A funny thing occurred during the Hawaii trip: My mom still looked very youthful in her 70's, Melissa was a mature college girl, and Dara was still in her pre-teens. No one could figure out if I was married to my mom or Melissa. Moreover, people wondered if Dara was Melissa's daughter. On a hike to Diamond Head some college students were overheard saying that Melissa was a "MILF." (Mom I'd Like To F**K). Melissa heard those students and made them very sorry they had opened their mouths.

A most hurtful thing during that time occurred when I took Dara to a gay group at Temple Valley Beth Shalom. Dara saw some men putting their arms around each other and giving non-sexual kisses and it shocked her. Soon after, I received a letter from Aileen's attorney indicating that they would initiate a restraining order if Dara were subjected to seeing anything related to a gay lifestyle. My attorney assured me that I was not subjecting Dara to anything that would hold up for a restraining order, but it still was like a knife wound for the fear of not being able to be with Dara in West Hollywood.

I also had a very close bond with Melissa at the time. Melissa was at the University of Arizona at Tucson, and I went up and visited her for a weekend in March 1996. I think we became very open and direct with each other about our feelings, and I felt closer with her then than ever before.

Evan remained very angry with me during most of the transitional years. While he said he could accept the "gay issue," he could not acknowledge the "deceptive issue." I know he felt very protective of his mom, and expressed his anger in an email he sent to his friend, Josh. He obviously felt very strongly about my being interested in other men while I was still married to his mother. And he felt the betrayal of his mother, the loss of security in his family, and confusion about knowing who I was.

My dad was still living during this time, but he had been diagnosed with Alzheimer's disease in the early 1990's. It had progressed slowly at first but then started to accelerate. In 1994, my dad had a caretaker helping at the Greenfield Avenue home. On October 8, 1995, my dad checked into the Jewish Home for the Aged, the same place where Bubbe spent her last years. My mom visited my dad each day, driving from West Los Angeles to Reseda.

I tried to come out to my dad, but he did not understand what I was saying. I will never know how he would have reacted if he had understood, but I do know, even if there were shock and disappointment, he still would have loved me and I believe it would have created more openness between us. I did ask my dad's best friend, Jack Levin, if my dad ever discussed with him the possibility that I might be gay. Jack said that he believes that my dad had no idea, and while he would have been surprised, it would not have changed the fact that he loved me.

I spent much of my time and energy during the transition years on working through the pending divorce. We had separated on July 19, 1995, and I hoped that the divorce would be resolved quickly since we both wanted it. However, the divorce proceedings took three years and were not finalized until May 1998. My lawyer was very qualified and had the same intent to conclude the proceedings as quickly as possible. There were no issues with dividing the community property equally. The major issue that extended the divorce proceedings was related to the sale of the business, which my parents had gifted to me as separate property. Finally, we resolved the differences and came to a compromise on the disputed items. Once the divorce became final, the healing began. While Aileen and I have not been friends since the divorce, we are friendly when we do see each other.

In 1996, I was still living in the apartment in Canoga Park. Driving around with Dara looking for a home to buy, we came across a house located at 932 N. Alfred Street, in West Hollywood. Dara wrote on a card, "Cute Little House." I bought that home, figuring I would fix it up and spend a couple of years living there before re-selling and moving elsewhere, which I did in 2018.

The Alfred Street house, built in 1923, became my own little universe. I fixed up the house over the years to be very comfortable and was really impressed with the results. Furnished in an eclectic style, it represents who I am. When people visit my home for the first time, I usually get a surprised response about how they never expected the plain simple home from the outside to reveal such an interesting and beautifully furnished house and gardens. I converted what was originally a garage into a cottage that I leased out.

At the time, I was living in both Palm Springs and West Hollywood. I would stay in West Hollywood primarily to visit family and friends, attend the theatre, and be able to have a place in the city when I wanted to be there. However, I did not like the traffic.

During these years, I began going to Palm Springs a couple of weekends each month. I was used to going there as my parents had owned a condominium in Palm Springs from the late 1960's. But I but never knew there was a large gay community there. In 1995 I rented an 800 square-foot apartment in Palm Springs. And in June of 1996, I purchased a condominium in the comfortable and affordable complex called Greenhouse East. It was a welcome upgrade to move from the small apartment to a 1400 square foot condominium with much nicer amenities.

During the transition years, I needed to become familiar with gay lifestyle. Additionally, I wanted to make up for the years of suppressing parts of myself and not experiencing gay culture. By 1998, I thought of myself more as "male attracted" than "gay." What I thought then was that although my sexual attraction was towards men, there was a lot in the gay culture that I did not identify with. The stereotype of going to bars and exclusively hanging around gay friends did not—and still does not—describe my identity; however, I needed to go through some of what I missed in early years.

I have to give myself credit for catching up quickly in acclimating myself to the new lifestyle. Once a neighbor was visiting me in my new home, and I was somewhat attracted to him, although he was quite a few years younger than I was. He candidly said, "Stan, you may be 52 years old, but you are only one gay year old. I may be 40, but I am 20 gay years old. I have no interest in dating a one gay year old because you will be experiencing a lot in the next few years and changing a lot yourself. You are not ready to even think of a relationship for the next couple of years because you need to grow up in gay years." He was so right, and even though I cannot even remember what he looks like today, I remember his words.

I did grow up and joined many gay groups so that I could be familiar with the gay community. I was informed about a Gay Fathers support group that met weekly and joined that immediately. I also joined The Valley Beth Shalom Temple group for gays, the Gay Gourmet. (I switched tables at each course, meeting 24 people during an evening), the Great Outdoors (gay hiking and travel excursions), Workshops (The Experience, Men's Journey, Married Gay Men, etc.), and the Internet sites and chat rooms for meeting other gay men. I would say that in three years of transition I grew to be at least 12 gay years old.

The Gay Fathers group met every Thursday night in Hollywood with a psychologist as the group leader. Many experienced Gay Fathers were there to support the new men who had recently come out and were dealing with issues similar to those I was dealing with. Most men dealt with recently coming out and how it affected their children and spouses. One of the problems that surprised me was that several men in the group were committed to staying married to their wives because they still loved each other, even though the man was gay. In spite of that, I knew that that it was best for Aileen and me to separate.

We discussed that, in my scenario, it seemed hardest for the children because they were dealing with both divorce and a gay dad. While being gay in the 1990's was becoming more socially acceptable, it still was unusual to have a gay dad. One of the Gay Fathers advised me, when I was talking about my kids, "You know, Stan, you've had 52 years to come to terms in one way or another with being gay. Remember this is all new to your kids. They have not even had six months to deal with this. They are being hurt by the family becoming a broken unit, and even issues of whether they should come out to their friends by saying they have a 'gay dad.' Just give them time and give them love." It was good advice which helped me get through some very difficult times.

I remember I was going to my psychologist Mike Silverman on a weekly basis. Finally, during a session in 1996, he said, "Stan, you don't need to come to me weekly anymore. You needed the therapy the most when you were married and hiding your sexuality and with your marriage problems with Aileen. Now, you are okay because you are who you are. You just need to come to me as needed." That is still the case today. I see Mike every once in a while, when there are issues that require some expert counseling and advice.

No one could ever guess who was one of my closest friends after I came out. It was my high school friend, Barbara Katz. We had maintained our friendship throughout the years. Barbi had many gay friends and was immediately accepting of me. It was comfortable to be with her, and we had a love for each other that continued. We went on trips together, most notably to San Francisco and New York. Barbi and I seemed to argue quite often, but it was a different kind of disagreement than what I experienced during my marriage. I liked that we argued without getting angry. Barbi gave up on trying to make me into a straight man as I decided that it was just too difficult to date women and men at the same time.

In 1996, I decided to try my hand again in retailing. The Ruggles Card & Gift shops had been closed for a number of years, and I was not interested in recreating that type of shop. Being close to the design area of Los Angeles, I leased a location on the corner of Melrose and San Vicente, across from the Pacific Design Center, and opened an "L shaped" store that had two entrances. One was called "Objets d'Art" and it connected inside to Decouverte Gallery for emerging artists.

The store featured home décor, unusual artsy types of gift items, and a small quality greeting card section. I thought the store would do well, being so close to the Pacific Design Center, but as I was setting up the store with Dara, we remember a man walking by and saying, "You will fail. Everyone else does here." What a bad omen! Although I was determined that would not happen, nevertheless, it failed. The problem was that it was on a busy corner where everyone passed by and did not stop to shop. Unfortunately, the clients going to the Pacific Design Center would rarely walk across the street to visit the shop.

We featured a couple of good artists that garnered attention, especially Steve Walker. He helped us earn four digits every day during his show. However, we barely covered the rent, and it was a financial loss. Everyone who came in loved the store, but it lacked foot traffic. The comment I heard most from people was "You should move your store to a mall or to Santa Fe. It would do so much better." Do you know the saying "location, location, location"? It was very apt for our situation. We closed after about one year, and it is now a restaurant.

1998 was significant because the divorce was finally settled, and I could move forward with my life. It was also the year marked by the death of my father on November 2, 1998, followed one week later by my mom's 80th birthday celebration. I was with my dad along with my mother and sister at the time that he passed away. When I remember my dad now, it was how he lived prior to getting Alzheimer's, when he was vibrant, intelligent, caring, and loving as a husband, father, and son.

932 Alfred Street, LA (1st Home after divorce) in 1996

CHAPTER 10

STANLEY PAPEL
THE LOST DECADE (1999–2009)

When we were married, Aileen and I had an unspoken arrangement. Aileen took care of the kids and the home, and I took care of the business and earning money.

Although ostensibly raising the kids was Aileen's domain, there were times when she wanted me to participate more in disciplining and parenting the children. Certainly, she encouraged this, but there were other times when she would criticize me when I tried to get more involved. My own lack of confidence as a Dad caused me to step back, which created more of a distance between the children and me.

I have such regrets now about the arrangement Aileen and I created. I wish I had been more involved with our children, and I wish Aileen had taken more responsibility beyond the household during our marriage. My mistakes can't be reversed, but hopefully I can make things better by taking responsibility for my decisions, right or wrong, and going forward.

Another defining mistake of my life was abdicating my position as head of Papel Giftware. It was a business I had received as a legacy from my father. I worked hard to expand the company and enjoyed seeing great success over the years, but after many years in charge I felt it was time to step back to a more minor role. I felt that the Company could retain the prominence it had and perhaps even increase in value if I would install someone as President of Papel Giftware until such time as another family member could step forward into the position, if they so desired.

I made the wrong choice for the CEO position. It was disastrous. Further, due to the new CEO's management style he caused a crisis which meant that in order to support him I was forced to betray a devoted, talented and loyal employee whom he simply could not get along with. Due to his management style and the choices he made, he contributed significantly to the downfall of Papel Giftware.

Does this sound familiar? It's the same mistake I made in my marriage. I abdicated my position as leader and ended up supporting decisions I felt were not the best, with results I ended up regretting. The result was another kind of divorce and the end of Papel Giftware. It was no longer the creation my Dad had left to me.

If I had not hired the CEO, and if I had not stepped back, Papel may still be operative today. Perhaps all my children would have had careers in the company. Maybe my sister Arlene would still be leading product development at Papel instead of at Ganz. We all have Papel in our blood, but there is no longer a Papel Giftware. This amounts to such a loss because Papel Giftware was more than just a company. It was a family which included many devoted, loyal and talented people who had also made careers of working with us at Papel. Unfortunately, that family is no longer around.

I count the choice of my partner, Steven Kent Chamberlain, as another major mistake in my life. But even with that wrong choice, I gained Kerry Chamberlain, who is truly like my third daughter.

As I look back on the "lost" decade, I wonder why Kent was my partner for 8 years of my life. I remember saying to Kent during the years 1999–2001 that these years with him were the best of my life. Admittedly, during the early years of our relationship, Kent brought me a lot of happiness. But as the years went by, and I discovered more about who he was, I have to wonder about my judgment in remaining in an unhealthy relationship. In contrast with Kent, Aileen has always been a person of high character. However, as with Aileen, I accepted living with Kent in an unhappy relationship.

Kent and I met online. From the moment we met on March 19, 1998, until we called each other partners, it was a very happy courtship. We had both been married for many years, and we both had children that we cherished. Kent was very handsome and outgoing, and once I met him, I did not want to date anyone else. We were exclusive with each other. Kent had previously sold his home and was renting a room with someone he worked with. When I invited Kent to "move in" on July 4, 1998, he accepted. We didn't call each other partners at that time; however, in time it developed into a partnership.

I had told Kent that I was in the final stages of a divorce, but the divorce had technically not been finalized. Kent told me that he was already divorced from his wife, Liz. Years later I found out that was not the case. Actually, at the time Kent and I met, he had only been separated without any divorce proceedings ever being initiated. I had told Kent my "coming out" story, and he told me that he had also come out to his two daughters, Kerry and Katie. This also was not true.

In 1998, Kent moved in with me in Palm Springs. I was finally happy after being alone for over 3 years from the time I separated from Aileen. My divorce was final, and both Aileen and I could go forward with our lives. Kent was so enjoyable to be with. We laughed. We enjoyed each other. I was truly happy. Life was good. I did not know at that time that Kent was untruthful. At the time, what I did not know did not hurt me.

Kent and I tried to meld our families: my children—Melissa, Evan and Dara—and Kent's daughters—Kerry and Katie. Dara enjoyed knowing Katie; she was like another big sister to her. Kerry and Melissa became very friendly and being the same age had a lot in common. Evan was the brother that Katie and Kerry never had before. I think my kids liked Katie and Kerry, but they had their reservations about Kent, long before I did.

There was a major emotional event in 1999. Kent had told me that he had come out to his kids, but they didn't talk about the "G" word (gay). When Dara and Katie were going to meet for the first time, Kent asked me not to discuss any "G" issues. I said that I would respect that, but I was not going to give any directives to Dara because she was only 13 years old and was dealing with enough at the time. However, when Dara and Katie met and became instant friends, Dara asked Katie, "How do you feel about your Dad being gay?" Katie said, "What? My dad isn't gay." Dara said, "What do you mean he isn't gay? They sleep in the same bed." This was a 13-year old talking to a 17-year old. I still feel terrible putting Dara through the ordeal of outing her dad and Kent to Katie. Kent had lied to me, and it resulted in hurting Dara and Katie. The problem was that I didn't realize that it should have been a warning sign that there were going to be problems ahead between Kent and me.

Kent and I took a trip to Cabo San Lucas one year to a deluxe timeshare with white sandy beaches and a full ocean view. Of course, we attended a timeshare presentation and ended up buying a timeshare, thinking how nice it would be to do family vacations together. It would be Melissa, Evan, Dara, Kerry and Katie with us for a week of bonding with the two dads.

Subsequently, I caught Kent not being truthful with me on several occasions, and by 2004 it became apparent that Kent and I were not compatible. The lying had eroded my trust in him, and once there was no trust, there was no reason to continue the relationship. We were going on a prescheduled cruise in August 2005, and I planned to spend the final day of the cruise discussing our next step with him—to end the relationship. I needed to let Kent know how I felt and that I wanted Kent to move out.

However, circumstances developed which induced me to hold off on having that discussion. Kent had been suffering from back pains for several months before the cruise. At first, he thought it was from lifting in the wrong way or a minor traffic accident that he had been in. As the pains continued, it seemed like something that could be more serious. A few days prior to the cruise, Kent's doctor referred him to an oncologist. It was the worst nightmare. Kent was diagnosed with Multiple Myeloma, which is cancer of the blood plasma. The cancer was attacking his spine and breaking his vertebrae. As a result, we canceled the cruise.

My energy needed to be focused on getting Kent through the crisis of the cancer. Personal matters were put in abeyance until Kent recovered. At first the chemo-therapy treatments were not successful, and the prognosis was not good for Kent surviving. He was in the most severe stage of Multiple Myeloma; the only therapy left was a stem cell transplant where they would culture his good blood cells and infuse that into his system. It worked and approximately one year after being diagnosed with cancer, he was considered to be cancer free. The extended recovery took its toll on Kent. He had been 6 feet, 1 inch before the cancer; the attack on his spinal cord left him the same height as me, 5 feet–8 inches. I knew he would continue needing chemotherapy each month so that the cancer would not return. It is truly a miracle, backed by his strong desire to live, that he survived this ordeal. Our relationship, however, did not survive. By December 2006 we officially separated as partners.

Kent asked that I not sell the house in Palm Springs. He wanted to lease the house from me, and he hoped to eventually buy the property. Without going into details, he violated the arrangement, and I felt no choice but to put the property on the market. His lack of character surfaced once again, and this time he threatened me, which was something I had never experienced before. It took the power of the lawyers and the involvement of police in order to settle the issues and for me to move forward. I was most thankful to be able to close this chapter of my life although I wondered about my blindness in not recognizing the problem for so many years. Kent passed away in 2012 when the cancer came out of remission.

After the breakup with Kent in December 2006 I dated some men exclusively for as long as a year. Some remained very dear friends that I hoped would be lifetime friends. However, there was no "Mr. Right." I resolved to myself that I might be without a soulmate during my lifetime. If that were the case, it would be okay. It would be better to have friends and happiness than to be unhappy in an unhealthy relationship. I was open to whatever would happen.

One of the most notable events at this time was Dara's Bat Mitzvah. Dara turned 13 on August 1, 1999, but her Bat Mitzvah was held at a beautiful country club on October 16, 1999. It was a themed event for the Oscars, and Dara was definitely the star. She looked so beautiful and did so well during the services. It was difficult for me to hold back my emotions; I knew how much difficulty Dara had gone through being affected by the divorce. For the Bat Mitzvah I pushed myself to do something which was a big step for me. I have the world's worst singing voice. I figured though, "if Dara can overcome all odds in pushing though her difficulties in life, I can at least push myself to sing a father's love song to Dara at her Bat Mitzvah." I took a singing class at Beverly Hills High School for over a year along with weekly private voice lessons. I persevered and, accompanied by a pianist, I sang my version of "I Don't Want to Miss a Thing"… originally sung by Aerosmith. I realized many years later that my singing embarrassed Dara. However, my intentions were good.

During those years there were trips with Dara as my joint custody included extended times during the summers. In 1999, Dara and I went together to Walt Disney World and Epcot Center. It was a bonding trip, especially at the Haunted Mansion attraction. I don't know who was more Dara or me, but we definitely were entertained. Dara also accompanied me a few years later in 2002 on a trip to Kent's family reunion in Grand Junction, CO. Dara was 15 ½ and had her driver's learning permit. My mom went with us on the trip, and Dara and Mom were roommates. Dara was in the midst of her teenage autonomy; she did her driver's training at the wheel through Boulder and Santa Fe. It was apparent that the "little girl" stages were no more. Dara and Grandma Sophie as roommates was really quite funny, as they bickered about my mom wanting the TV turned off while Dara was adamant about staying up late. Later that year, Dara turned Sweet 16!

The most exciting family events during the first decade of this new century was Melissa's marriage to Gregg Moscot on November 13, 2004, and then the birth of my first granddaughter, Lily Josephine Moscot, on June 6, 2007.

Melissa and Gregg Moscot. Wedding in 2004

Stanley Papel and Kent Chamberlain in 2004

Dara Papel. Bat Mitzvah in 1999

Dara Papel. Bat Mitzvah in 1999

CHAPTER 11

STANLEY PAPEL

THE CAREER YEARS (1970–2014)

Author's Note: The complete career for both Phil Papel and Stan Papel is contained in a draft version of a book completed in 2018 titled Tales Beyond Main Street. *In addition, an out-of-print book titled* Little Shop on Main Street, *by author and Disney historian Dave Mason, shares the story of Ruggles China & Gift Shop on Main Street, U.S.A. at Disneyland (1955–1964). Some of the content in this chapter has been covered in earlier chapters. Readers already familiar with these stories may opt to continue to Chapter 12.*

When I joined the Ruggles in 1970, sales were just over one million dollars and Papel sales were about $750,000; our wholesale sales were significantly less than the total sales volume of our retail stores. Furthermore, nearly half of the sales of Phil Papel imports were resold to our own Ruggles retail stores in 1970. At that stage, only about three hundred fifty thousand dollars of Phil Papel Imports was sold to non-Ruggles retail stores.

By 1972, I was starting to make business trips on my own. I'll never forget the first trip I booked from LA to Tokyo. It was with a charter airline for some crazy low price like $500. I didn't realize that the route was Los Angeles to San Francisco, with the next stop in Seattle, then on to Anchorage, then to Seoul, and finally to Tokyo Haneda Airport about 36 hours later. I never did that again. As I made more trips to Asia, I began to see the opportunities to easily develop our own product. We did this first on Japanese porcelain and used decals manufactured in the United Kingdom by Matthey Bishop, which was, at the time, the best decals maker supplying the finest companies in the UK on bone china and porcelain. We would import the decals from Matthey Bishop and then ship them over to Japan. I was going 4 times a year to Japan at the time, and would often load my suitcases up with decals in order to save shipping costs. I'd haul these 100 pound suitcases around until I got to my agent in Nagoya, Japan. That was before they had wheels on suitcases.

Most of our importing from Asia was handled through a company called Dorna Trading Company. When I first started working at Papel, my dad had me to work with "Frank" at Dorna Trading. We had imported primarily non-exclusive items at the time, but they were good sellers as selected by my dad and they had exceptional margins. At the time their Yen was fixed at ¥240 to the USD $1.00. (Today there are less than ¥100 yen to the USD $1.00!) During my first trip to Japan, I met Frank. To my shock, Frank was a woman! Her English name was Bessie Miyake. She told me than women in Japan weren't respected as business directors; that is why she said her name was Frank. However, after the first meeting, she gave me permission to call her Bessie. I worked with Bessie for many years, at first picking factory items but then working towards exclusive product as the line developed.

Developing new exclusive products became a passion. One category that I was very proud of developing was the collector thimbles back in the mid-late 70's. They were already becoming collectors' items from Europe. I would get these small bit decals and have them applied to porcelain thimbles made in Japan. The cost of goods was about USD $0.11. The thimble was about USD $0.10 and the decal was less than $0.01. Final cost after freight and duty the thimbles were about USD $0.13. Papel set the wholesale price of the thimbles at USD $1.00 and they normally retailed for about USD$2.98. Papel sold many with a gross margin of nearly 8 times cost. It was the beginning of our company establishing a strong cash reserve. We developed an entire line of miniatures by the mid-1970 with margins on the other items that were often tripling or quadrupling our costs! Needless to say, our profitability started to grow, as well as our customer base nationwide.

However, our true success and the beginning of our becoming a nationally recognized company happened in 1976. It's a combination of factors, and I am grateful to this day for the sequence of events that led to the major change in our company.

By 1976 all locations of Ruggles Queen Mary were open and operative. Our #1 selling item was a Name Mug program that depicted the Queen Mary along with 180 popular first names. Papel had the decals printed in the UK by Matthey Bishop, and the mugs were manufactured and decorated in Ohio by a company called Scio. We were retailing over 100 mugs or more each per day.

My dad said to me. "Stan, why don't we just add the Matthey Bishop flowers for the girl's names and old-fashioned automobiles for the men's names? Then we can make it part of the wholesale line." Virginia's Gift Shop in Knott's Berry Farm added them and literally could not keep them in stock Virginia's would order 6 mugs with the same name, and often they were sold out of that name in one day.

I had kept in touch with Henry Sulzberger, who was the Divisional Merchandise Manager at May Company. I said, "Mr. Sulzberger, I think we have another Deltress wigs on our hands." Henry said, "Stan, I want to try the mugs in the downtown store in the Stationery Department" The same thing happened. They absolutely could not keep them in stock. The cost of the Name Mugs at the time was $12/dozen. Retail at first was $1.99. May Company added them to all the stores in Southern California and soon expanded nationally. We just could not supply them fast enough. We had to cut off all new accounts but tried to keep as many of the card and gift shops supplied because they were our account base. Scio could not keep up with us, and we began ordering the mug bodies from Japan. Then, we ordered our first kiln and started decorating the ceramic bodies ourselves. We had the 1-color name decals printed in the USA; however, our designed decals all came from Matthey Bishop, Inc. Soon Papel outgrew the first warehouse we owned in Los Angeles. We rented an adjacent warehouse across the street just to store the undecorated and decorated name mugs.

Within one year, Papel's sales went from eight hundred thousand dollars per year to over three million dollars. We were decorating on 3 shifts of 8 hours a day, 7 days a week, and we still could not keep up with the supply. Within a year there were knock-offs which ate into our business, but we were still the leader and by then we were adding new decorative designs to the name mugs. I remember getting a photo from one lady who bought about 15 mugs with her first name, all with different designs. We added to the mug line a "World's Greatest" series of over 75 designs, a "Kiss Me" series of over 75 designs, and later a Dog and Cat breed mug series of over 50 breeds. At one point we were receiving as many as six or seven 40-foot containers a month of mugs. Each container was about 60,000 mugs. We were the talk of South Central Los Angeles.

My dad and mom had been enjoying their Palm Springs life, which started originally from Thursday to Monday of each week. However, my dad started coming in to work less and less, although he always enjoyed the industry gift shows and sharing his valued input as Chairman of the Board. My sister, Arlene Slater, began with the company just as a part-timer, writing our monthly Newsletter. Once we got into decorating the name mugs, we began getting a lot of inquiries for Custom Design. This meant having Name Mugs with souvenir logos and designs that were specifically created for a tourist location. Then, the area of custom design expanded into several mugs which included the first mug for Apple, which is now an eagerly sought collectible.

By 1978, we were in 4 warehouses located within two city blocks in South Central LA. We had outgrown all of our premises. Even more concerning was the safety issues for our employees due to the danger in the area with so much crime. The breaking straw was that our retail offices at the location were being serviced by many salespeople and vendors. We had credit cards, then called BankAmericards, at all our stores. Our front door was safety locked and required visitors to be buzzed in. We once opened the door for the BankAmericard representative and she was covered in blood, her beautiful clothes all torn. Two men had tried to grab her purse, and she wouldn't let go of it. She was dragged a full block until they finally pried the purse from her. We decided then it was time to move and began the search for a single building that would hold our offices and warehouse.

My dad had been successful in all his real estate ventures, and he took on the challenge of finding a new home for Papel. He searched primarily in the San Fernando area since warehouse property was still within an affordable rate compared to the Los Angeles area. After a few months of searching and negotiations Phil found a beautiful building near a nice residential area in North Hollywood, located about a 30-minute drive northwest of the warehouses in South Central Los Angeles. The building was just over 100,000 square feet, which included nearly 10,000 square feet of office space. It was actually more space than we needed but gave us room to grow. The back 30,000 square feet were leased out for the first couple of years. The building became the new home for Papel and was a very wise investment.

Our staffing and product line continued to grow once we relocated to our new premises in North Hollywood, CA. We added a Human Resources department under the direction of Jo Lewis. She was excellent. The marketing department grew with the addition of John Allenberg, who was a major contributor to the growth of Papel, especially in the sports related markets.

Papel had secured the license to the 1984 Summer Olympics in early 1980, which was a real bonanza for the company. The license required a guaranteed royalty of four hundred thousand dollars, which seemed like a lot of money at the time. Each year, my workload seemed to be become heavier, and I was pulled between trying to develop new products and the administration of a growing company. When I would go on trips, there were more often than not administrative problems needing to be resolved. Therefore, in 1981, I made the decision to look for a new company president so I could concentrate on the development of new product and oversee the marketing functions.

The biggest mistake I made in my business career was the selection I made for our company president. I must hold myself accountable for the outcome because I was the majority shareholder of the company and held the power to overrule any decisions he made. However, the company lost millions of dollars due to his bad judgment. He made inventory purchases to support projected sales that never materialized. He simply did not have a good sense of what products would sell and how to gauge the market. I would have been better off making those decisions myself, but at the time I was overwhelmed with other duties I was responsible for. I had to depend on him, but my trust was misplaced. I suppose we all find ourselves needing to trust people who in the end disappoint us; it's part of life. In the 3 years he was there we went from a company that had significant cash reserves to being in debt to the tune of over $5,000,000 with sales of approximately $12,000,000 a year at the time.

At the time our new president was hired, our sales were $7,000,000, with most of those sales being in mugs, but with a growing segment in concepts such as Midlife Crisis / Over-the-Hill, Golf gifts, seasonal gifts such as Valentine's Day and Mother's Day, and our souvenirs and custom designs. We had just been awarded the 1984 Los Angeles Olympics category for the ceramics and glass categories based upon our reputation and being a Los Angeles-based decorator in both ceramic and glass. It was Phil Papel's personal reputation that secured the license. Our new president indicated that this project would be "his baby" and that he would leave the mugs and general gifts to me. Papel did develop a beautiful line of Olympic designs, which can be viewed on our website www.papelgifts.com. The problem occurred when our president made major commitments to factories in the Japan and Korea with quantities far beyond our sales level. My dad and I had a more conservative approach of ordering white ware and decorating to meet demand, even if it was 3 shifts of 8 hours. However, our president made purchasing commitments for shipments in 1984 that far exceeded our actual sales. Retailers did not want to be stuck with inventory after the Olympics, so Papel ended up having to liquidate over $1,000,000 at cost of obsolete inventory. Our sales of Olympic product were four million dollars at wholesale. It was disheartening because along with the increased expenses related to staffing and an advertising campaign, we went from a positive cash flow to needing to borrow significant sums from the bank.

The Olympics did result in good additional licenses though. We secured the licenses for ceramic and glass for the NFL, MLB, NBA and NHL which were well marketed by John Allenberg, and which became an important part of our sales after 1984.

Concurrently, our "Greeting Mugs—A Greeting Card with a Handle" sold over one million dollars per year, and we attained excellent licenses such as Blue Mountain Arts and Flavia as well as many other greeting card lines that we translated onto mugs. It was a great program that lasted for years. We continually would change the designs on the program to keep the look fresh for both retailers and consumers.

Each year I would do two shows in Europe: one in Birmingham, England, and the other in Frankfurt, Germany. In 1983 I saw a series of ceramic tiles that could be used as a permanent Greeting Card. I felt that it was a natural for Papel. With all of the greeting card licensees, it seemed it could turn into a major greeting card-gift category.

Our president loved the Forever Card idea. But he said that from now on I should handle mugs since it was a "no brainer." However, as president, he would take on the responsibility of coordinating the Forever Card program. I would report to him and submit the designs for his approval. He mandated that he would do all the marketing and sourcing.

To make a long story short, the program did not go over the way our president had envisioned. To many consumers and retailers, it looked like just a decorated tile and the ceramic greeting card aspect did not catch on. Finally, we introduced a 24-facing program, but it did not come anywhere near meet to volume that warranted a one million-piece commitment. So, in 1985 we lost another $1,000,000 due to purchases and expenses that were out of control. As a result of these failures and miscalculations, I terminated the employment of our company president at the end of 1985.

In the following year, we turned the company around from losing over $1,000,000 in 1985 to making a $100,000 profit in 1986 including the interest expense to the bank of over $500,000. In other words, Papel went from an operating loss of one million dollars per year in 1984 and 1985 to an operating profit of six hundred thousand dollars in 1986. However, the uncertainty and high debt owed to the bank placed my family and me in a financially precarious position. The financial liabilities in the preceding 3 years resulted in a change that put Papel on a different course forever. Realizing the company's high debt that the company meant a need for major changes in the future. Thus, a new chapter began for Papel Giftware.

In 1986, before I sold the company to Russ Berrie, I was considering hanging on for a while longer. After all, we had gone from a 7-digit loss in 1985 to a 6-digit gain in 1986. However, Russ talked me out of holding onto the company. He was the world's best salesman. Russ said, "What if the bank calls the loan, which was a real possibility, or what if interest rates spiked back up to 18%?" Russ said I had already proved that I could make a company successful, and his company would take Papel to the next level by improving sales, finances and operations. They would leave the Product Development to Arlene and me. Papel needed help in the other areas, but the product line was our strength. Russ wanted to increase their market share by buying Papel. RUSS finally got Papel in 1987. However, it was a very short honeymoon.

There were ongoing tensions between Russ and me primarily related to my awareness that there were inconsistencies in the cost of goods coming from their overseas buying offices. RUSS was listed on the NYSE as a publicly traded company. I felt it was my responsibility to show proof that there was a significant difference between what Papel was paying and the prices originally quoted, which basically meant that staff in their overseas offices were padding the prices and the price difference was going into someone else's pockets. When I provided documentation to top management of the

Papel Giftware Trade Show circa 1983

inconsistencies in the pricing, I was told that I should keep out of the affairs in the foreign offices.

To make matters worse, a management employee who left RUSS was beaten up and attacked by unknown assailants in Hong Kong. I was told by one of our suppliers that it was known I was "too close" to uncovering what was going on, and that it was very possible I could also be in danger if I continued to convey the information that I knew. I did not tell anyone but my wife, but it was enough for me to step back. I did not even tell my sister, who worked closely with our VP of Overseas Operations and was on very good terms with him. I figured I would just complete my three-year commitment to work for Papel, and then would figure out what my next step should be. This gift industry was not so beautiful after all. What had I gotten myself into?

Russ continued to be derogatory to me in his conversations, but it didn't have much effect on me because I knew my future was not going to be with Russ after 1990. Russ once gave me a back-handed compliment. He said, "The one good thing about you is that you have a sense of urgency." I think that what he meant was everything else about me was bad. We did have a few discussions about the importance of new product vs. sales. I told him I believed they were both equally important. He said that sales happen if you have a good sales force and decent product. He said ideas are not original in the sense that every idea comes from something else that is already there. I do believe that he did respect some of the unique concepts originated by Arlene and me. I know that both Russ and our VP of Overseas Operations liked and respected my sister. She was being trained to take over my role as heading Product Development, and I was happy about that because she wanted that role.

Years after Russ died, I asked wife, Angelica, if he had ever talked about me to her and if he disliked me. Angelica said that he didn't dislike me. I told her that I had never really thanked Russ for buying Papel, and I felt badly that we never had closure on some of our heated exchanges. Russ definitely taught me that it is a jungle out there, even in the giftware industry. Before I met him, I thought that Product was the driving force in the Giftware Industry. I learned from Russ Berrie that Sales, not Product, drives the industry.

Also, I don't want to come across as if everything was negative during the time with Russ. He had some amazing people in his organization that resulted in major achievements for Papel and brought new contacts to me that would have never happened if it were not for Russ. The international organization included several very strong fans of Papel. Papel was already very well established in the UK with sales over $1,000,000 at the time I sold to Russ Berrie and Company. However, within a couple of years, I believe our UK sales reached over USD $8 million, which was amazing growth. Our international sales in many countries reached new heights, and I had a very positive professional working relationship with several of the talented sales personnel with Russ Berrie and Company.

In June 1989, which was 6 months prior to the end of the 3-year employment contract, Russ and I came to terms for my early departure. I was paid my salary through the end of 1989, but I was basically unemployed in the wholesale giftware industry. I still had ownership of the Ruggles retail stores, but they were so well managed by our General Manager, Ruth Donley, that I had very little to do.

Since I had a non-compete clause in the giftware industry for 3 years, I decided to develop new products which could be licensed. Thus, instead of importing products directly, I owned the designs and licensed them for a royalty to numerous major companies in the industry.

I decided to lease an office and showroom near my home located in Encino, California, which was literally 3 blocks away from where I lived and I would walk to my office each day. I hired an administrative assistant, Barbara Starr, who had previously worked at Papel. I also hired two Product Development Managers to help put the line together. Ruth Donley, in addition to being the General Manager of Ruggles, also worked as Controller for the new Papel Designs. Within two years, we had licensed to eight major importers in the USA as well as offered designs through UK, Canada, Australia, New Zealand and South Africa. By 1998, I had adjusted to my "new life" and business was back on track with an excellent group of companies licensing from Papel Designs. In 1999

Kent and I took a trip to Australia where Papel Designs had excellent distribution through a company called Skansen. Skansen was selling socks with expressions on them, similar to what we had sold on mugs. I decided to do use the same concept on developing a line of personalized name socks as well as socks with social and personal expressions. From 1998–2002, Papel Designs began importing and selling these types of socks, which we imported from Korea and wholesaled from our offices and warehouse in Palm Springs. Our sales were about $1,000,000 per year by 2002, and it seemed like we were going to be on track for growth. However, the world was a lot different in 2002 than it was when I was in business in back in the 1980's. $1,000,000 in sales for a start-up company sounded like it would be healthy, but with our expense structure it was unprofitable.

Eventually we closed the operation and rolled our company into Papel Giftware, which was now owned by Cast Art. Cast Art then ended up closing their operations, so we then returned to licensing our designs to major giftware companies. The licensing continued until 2018, at which time my licensing of new products was discontinued. Melissa has continued licensing her new designs on mugs under her business name, M. Papel Designs. My son Evan started his own company called Pocket Socks where he developed a line of Zipper socks which were originally related to a line of socks from Papel Designs. So, in those ways the company lives on.

The Pink Panther Story

A favorite business-related story has to do with "The Pink Panther" (1964), a comedy film directed by Blake Edwards. For those not old enough to remember, the film featured David Niven, Peter Sellers and Robert Wagner, along with memorable opening credits featuring animation of the title character. The movie was successful and the stuffed animal of the Pink Panther was a popular seller in our retail stores. The sizes of the stuffed animals varied from about 8 inches all the way to 6 feet. The 6-foot Pink Panther sold for $300, which was a lot of money back in late sixties. During Christmas time the sales peaked, and we would have one or two Pink Panthers in each of mall store locations, plus we would keep a backup of about six Pink Panthers in the warehouse so that we could supply the stores as needed. If we sold the last Pink Panther in any of the stores, it would prohibit us from selling future 6-foot Pink Panthers during the busy Christmas Season.

During the Christmas seasons while the character was most popular, it would be my "job" to deliver Pink Panthers to the various shops, primarily at Fox Hills Mall, Glendale Galleria, and the Bonaventure Hotel. The easiest way to deliver, especially if I had two of them, was to put one of them in the passenger side of the front seat (using the seat buckle) and the second one in the back seat also buckled in.

Can you imagine what attention I got as I was driving the Pink Panthers to the stores? Everyone was looking and laughing and I also kept on laughing. By the time I got to the stores, my stomach would be aching from the amount of laughing I did. I wonder in today's age if that would have gotten me into the fast lane of the freeway requiring two or more in the passengers in a vehicle!

The Charms Of Bonaventure Hotel

Our largest store in the Ruggles chain, after the closing of the shop on the Queen Mary, was the 3500 square foot location on one of the mezzanine levels of the Bonaventure Hotel in downtown Los Angeles. The store was run by Jean Mack at the time, one of our very capable managers. Due to the size of this store location not only did we offer our normal gift and card shop choices, but also expanded this store to include a jewelry and accessories department as well as a ready-to-wear clothing department.

In our jewelry department we offered gold plated charms of the Bonaventure Hotel for $4.00 each. Can you imagine the surprise of our manager, Jean Mack, when a very wealthy Arab came up to the jewelry counter and pulled out $1600 in $100 bills? He pointed to the gold-plated charms and said that he would take four of them. Jean was taken aback, but she still said, "Thank you, Sir, but those are $4.00 not $400 each". He gave her a surprised look, picked up his $1600 dollars, said, "Then, I don't want them," and walked out.

The Famous Ruggles Dollar Table

Back in the days of our gift shops in Disneyland and the Disneyland Hotel, my dad had what was called the Grab Bag. This was a large barrel that contained boxed items that were packed in various colored bags. Back in 1955 they sold for 59-cents with the captions, "Odds much better than Las Vegas" and "Values to $5." It was our number one selling item. My sister Arlene Slater's job in those days was to wrap the grab bags. A few years later we increased the price to 79-cents and sales were not negatively affected at all.

When we opened the retail stores in other locations, we did not want to go to the labor of having to make sure every item was boxed and then to wrap each item individually; therefore, to replace the Grab Bag concept, we replaced it with the Dollar Table. Initially most of the items on the dollar table were items that originally retailed for $2–$3 but were marked down because they were slow sellers. However, sometime in the 1960's and 1970's as we became known for our Dollar Table, we started to buy close-outs and put them out for $1, which was a great deal! I sometimes think back and say to myself, "This Dollar Table was so popular. Why didn't we make an entire store of dollar items, like today's so successful 99-Cent Stores or Dollar Tree?"

CHAPTER 12

STANLEY PAPEL
TRAVEL (1945–2019)

I've always had a passion for travel. It's February 12, 2013, and I am on the third day of a safari at a camp called Tsakane in Kruger Park, South Africa. The camp is very basic, quite a bit different than what I had expected. I am traveling with a companion, Jose Islas, on a trip that will cover not only the Safari but also Johannesburg, Cape Town, and the Garden Route. It's been one of the trips I have wanted to do while I am still able to travel easily. I am getting to a stage in life where I like comforts, and this camp is a little more "basic" than what I had originally anticipated. Yet, when it is over, I will look back and be glad that I traveled this way.

If I ever do another safari it will be more secure with more comforts. There isn't any protection surrounding the camp, and I have been told that lions have come into the campgrounds at night. Yesterday we got very close to a giraffe, and it is exhilarating to see such a beautiful animal in the wild and up close. The giraffe seemed as interested in us as we were in him. This morning, after getting up around 5:30 am, the guide brought us to a section of the camp where we were able to see a beautiful male elephant up close. If we were not on a deck, we would have been too close for safety. It was almost as if the elephant was posing for us—front view, drinking water and lifting his trunk, then turning around so that we could see him from all angles. On the safari later in the morning, we came upon a herd of over 100 buffalos. These are not like the ones in the USA, and they do charge at people including when in vehicles. The safari vehicle got stuck in the sand earlier in the morning, and I was truthfully fearing for my safety as the herd got close to the vehicle.

Back in 2011, I visited several European cities including London, Stockholm, Warsaw, Krakow, Rome. A later visit to Europe in 2012 included London, Lisbon and Paris. With several excursions along the way, I came home absolutely exhausted Yet, it was my choice to see a lot and to do this type of adventurous travel. I had no regrets, but I began to realize that it might be time to slow down a bit and come home relaxed rather than to need another vacation just to recover.

In my most active working years in the 70's and 80's, I would travel to Asia as many as four times a year, plus visit London at least once each year, and then travel to Gift Shows throughout the world.

When I separated from Aileen in 1995, I continued to have the desire to travel. When I was partnered with Kent Chamberlin, from 1998–2006, we took several domestic and international trips as well as my continuing the business trips to Asia each year.

There were many memorable travels throughout my life. I have probably done more traveling than 90% of the people my age. There are very few places that I have wanted to go but haven't been to yet. I'd like to visit Istanbul. I'd also like to take more cruises, and revisit some of my favorite world destinations such as Brazil and Israel.

I would break my life travel into 4 groupings:

1. Before marriage (1945–1972)

My first major solo trip was in the summer of 1961 in Hawaii for about 8 weeks. There wasn't a lot of travel once I was in Hawaii, but the experience of being on my own and enjoying a beautiful environment awakened me to the fun of being away and in a different habitat. I took classes for 6 weeks. My parents and Arlene joined me in Hawaii at the end of my stay. I went from student accommodations to luxury at the Hilton Hawaiian Village. I remember that my dad paid $40 for the room, which was a lot of money in those days. This was followed by a visit to Kauai for our stay at the iconic Coco Palms Resort (site of filming that same year for the Elvis Presley film, "Blue Hawaii").

My second major trip was in 1962, which was more than just a trip. I drove to Mexico and took classes at the University of the Americas in Mexico City for about 5 months.

The third, and by far the most exciting trip probably in my entire life, was in 1967 after I received my master's degree and traveled with two friends, one met along the way, from Denmark all the way down to Israel. While on that trip I collected coins from the many countries I visited and have given that collection to my granddaughter, Lily.

Other "before marriage" trips that I also enjoyed were:

The first trip I can remember, to Palm Springs, with my parents when I was only 3 years old.

The many, many trips to Las Vegas with my parents and sister over many years. We used to stay at the Flamingo Hotel, and I remember my Dad giving big tips, like $5, so that we would have good seats for the dinner shows.

A trip to Yosemite as a family in 1954 where stayed in a cabin at Camp Curry.

2. During marriage (1972–1995)

Several trips that stand-out, the most momentous being the return from Asia that resulted in Dara being "conceived."

I thoroughly enjoyed the trip to Israel with Aileen, Melissa, and Evan in 1987.

A trip that Aileen and I took to England and Netherlands early in our marriage. Another to the USSR while it was still behind the Iron Curtain. This was certainly an eye opener for both Aileen and me. I remember they opened the first McDonalds in the USSR while we were there, and there were long lines of people waiting over an hour to get a taste of a McDonalds burger and fries. Of course, Aileen and I did not wait in line for that. I do remember the conditions being very Third World in terms of hotels and restaurants.

Among the trips during marriage that I would put near the top were the many cruises sponsored by my dad and mom that included our family and the Slaters; eleven of us in all. It became a very special bonding time for our family. I think there were at least six cruises that we all took together. The last one was in February 1995 when my dad was already in the advanced stages of Alzheimer's. We included a caretaker on that trip, but it was obvious that it would be the last cruise that we would ever take as a family of eleven.

There were many business trips during this time that I also enjoyed. Of course, I liked being in business and making headway on new products. While travel to Asia became somewhat repetitive after so many trips, going to new destinations was always fun, especially to Brazil and Chile. Papel Giftware imported products from both countries for several years during the 1980's.

I also enjoyed the trips to Europe that were business-based. For the bi-annual trade show in Birmingham, UK, I would stay in London and take the train each day and evening back-and-forth. I would take in the London theatre every night, which made the trip both business and pleasure. Papel's business operations were very strong in the UK, so I enjoyed being at the trade shows and working with the people that ran the Papel freelance operation in the UK and Europe.

My other favorite business destinations were Hong Kong and Thailand. I became close with the people I worked with in Bangkok. Hong Kong was always a bustling and exciting city.

One of the most memorable trips that I took was the 10 day trek in Nepal in 1994, following a business trip to Bangkok. It was preceded by a 3-day stay in a jungle resort on the border of Nepal and India. It was a physical challenge, but the trip was also mentally engaging. It was during the breaks each day that I began writing my life story. It was also when I came to terms with the unhappiness in my marriage and with my sexuality. I would call this the most life changing trip of my life since I separated from Aileen and came out in less than a year.

3. After Marriage (1995–2006)

Between 1995- 1998 travel was not a priority in my life. Most of the trips that I recall involved weekends in Palm Springs. As a matter of fact, I travelled between Los Angeles and Palm Springs so often that I decided to buy a condo in Palm Springs in 1996 because owning a place seemed a lot more practical than paying for hotels.

I also scheduled a gay cruise in February 1996. The strange thing is that it was the same exact ship and destinations that I had taken with my family in February 1995. I even recognized some of the staff, but certainly the experience was completely different than what I experienced only one year earlier. It was an amazing amount of fun to be on a ship with 2,000 gay men. One funny thing is that a year earlier, Aileen and I had been telling Melissa and Evan to be back in our stateroom by 2 a.m. since we retired earlier. Now I was the one staying out late—and really catching up for the years that I missed by not coming out earlier in life.

I do remember also frequenting Santa Fe during those years, at least once a year. I enjoyed the good food, art, and the relaxation. It was a place where I would reflect on life. I bought several pieces of art, some of the best I own, from Santa Fe, which I hope will remain in my family.

Other vacations during this time period were taken primarily with Dara, to Washington, DC, to Orlando, and to San Francisco. I also enjoyed a very special trip to Hawaii with my mom, Melissa, and Dara.

During these years, I started acquiring timeshares at Carlsbad, Del Mar and Laguna Beach, all of which I have now sold. I still retain and enjoy scheduled getaways at the San Francisco timeshare.

My outlet for getting my mind off my problems or, perhaps, for reflecting about my life, has always been travel. I unofficially started a "bucket list" of places I wanted to visit, or re-visit.

4. Single Again (2006–2019)

In 2007, I took a group tour to Israel, Jordan, and Egypt. Funny thing is that I have been to Israel on three occasions: 1967 as a student; 1987 as a family man; and 2007 as a gay man. It seemed that the country had changed as much in the past twenty years as I had! I wonder if I will go back in 2027 as a very old man, just to keep the pattern going. Well, I doubt that. Still, I enjoyed Israel very much each time, and in different ways. I also was glad I went to Egypt, but I have no desire to ever go back there. Seeing the relics of such an historic civilization was amazing. I enjoyed visiting Jordan very much also. I hadn't gone there with any expectations, but I found the people very friendly and the lifestyle to be so respectful.

Through the years, I have enjoyed travel with several of my friends. I've traveled with David Jones to Thailand, including the Northern Thailand and Golden Triangle area that touched 3 countries; to Vietnam with Toby Cooper; and to Cambodia with Denis McDougal.

I think I have been to Europe many times since 2007, often alone but often meeting friends along the way. Countries that I visited in Europe in the last few years included the England, Scotland, Ireland, N. Ireland, Sweden, Denmark, Belgium, Netherlands, France, Spain, Germany, Poland, Hungary, Czech Republic, Slovakia, Austria, Hungary and Italy. There were certain benefits of being solo traveler and also drawbacks. For me, the sad part happened when I was enjoying something very much, such as theatre or a good meal, and I had no one to share the experience with. However, I also have such fond memories of people I have met as a single man. That would not have happened if I were with a partner.

There are also certain places in the USA that I have repeatedly revisited which represent special occasions in life. San Francisco is one of my favorite cities, and I just do the same things each time I visit. Of course, I am doing new things along the way, but I walk the same route each trip, and usually eat at many of the same restaurants. I think I have owned the timeshare in San Francisco for 30 years, and I never tire of the city. One funny thing, as you probably know, San Francisco is very hilly. I always walk to Fisherman's Wharf from my hotel and then walk around the Embarcadero to the Terminal Building (Pier 1) and then back on Market Street to my hotel. Each trip it takes a little longer than the time before, and I keep saying that they are making the hills steeper in San Francisco each trip. I think I can still make that same walk for another 10 years, but it is going to take longer and longer each time.

Another favorite place for me is Hawaii. I typically visit Waikiki on Oahu, but I also visit the other islands on occasion. I've made some wonderful friends in Hawaii over the years, and I enjoy the beauty, rest and relaxation of the Islands. It is also a place where I revisit and do some of the same things over and over. The waitresses often remember me at the restaurants and a couple of the staff members still know me at the Princess Kaiulani which has been the usual place where I've stayed for the past several years. I am ready for a change of hotels though, but I will keep visiting Hawaii.

I often visit New York for about 5 or 6 nights each year. I see theatre each day or night and also have a few favorite restaurants. I'm close to my cousins, Nancy and Arnold Koopersmith and often spend an over-night at their home. I'm also close to Teddie (Theodora) and Joel Moscot, who are my son-in-law Gregg's aunt and uncle. They have been very welcoming of me as family, which has meant a lot to me. Both the Koopersmiths and the Moscots are so much fun to be with that it is a highly anticipated part of every visit to New York.

I haven't been back often to Asia as I went there so often for business during my career. At some point, I would like to visit Thailand again.

South Africa will stand out as one of the most memorial trips of my life. After the safari, I returned to Johannesburg for a few more days and then continued on to Cape Town with a 4-day group tour called the Garden Route. Each night was a different location and the drive gave us the opportunity to see much more of the countryside.

Cape Town was a highlight and one of my favorite world cities. One funny experience (not so funny at the time) was when our shuttle from the airport to the hotel ran out of gas. We had to pull over and wait while the driver who went on foot to find gas. As an offset to the problem, the hotel upgraded us to their master suite. It was the nicest room I have ever had in my life—probably about 2500 sq. ft. While in Cape Town, we met Pam and Izzy Roseman, who are Nev Roseman's uncle and aunt (Nev and Rita Roseman are the parents of my son Evan's wife, Deborah Roseman Papel). Our room at a gay-friendly hotel was beautifully decorated and our friends enjoyed a quick tour of our suite. They loved it along with some of the "eye candy" that caught the attention of Nev's relatively young aunt. Another highlight of the trip was meeting some of my cousins in Johannesburg, especially my cousin Kerry and her lovely mother Chloe Simon, who were so welcoming that I immediately felt that I had known them forever.

As I age, I find that my preference is to do fewer international trips with the exception of easy travel without a lot of destinations. In the summer of 2016, I took a trip to London, Munich, and Berlin, destinations that I have been to before but had a desire to see again. Berlin was especially interesting because my many trips before took place when the wall was up, and I had to go through "Checkpoint Charlie" to get into the eastern side. By 2016, the Berlin Wall was down, and I experienced one beautifully integrated city. London has always been a favorite city, and I enjoy the theatre there even more than in New York.

Also, one of the most memorable travel periods of my life occurred between August 7 and October 4, 2018. I call it my "Vagabond Travels." In early August, I received a phone call that a continual stream of water was coming out of my condo in West Hollywood. I authorized entry, and it turned out that there was a sewage backup in my bottom floor unit that came down from the units on the upper stories. The Homeowners Association had not flushed the pipes between the units, which resulted in sewage coming out through my toilet and shower, which eventually covered the bathroom, bedroom, closets, hallway and living room. There soon developed a dispute between my insurance company and the HOA's insurance company of responsibility for the repairs. Meanwhile, my living expenses would be covered during the repair period, except for the time I spent in Palm Springs because I owned a home there. Since it was summertime, I had no desire to be in Palm Springs when I could be covered for hotel and meals when I travelled elsewhere.

I had only recently retired and thought it would be fun to be a "vagabond" until the condo was repaired. I was going to start a driving trip and only plan one day in advance of where I would end up the following day. I wanted to see parts of California in ways that I had never seen it before. Usually I am a very structured person; now, I would be carefree and just enjoy each day without a plan.

The time started off very exciting. I spent the first few days in Santa Barbara and then went on to Pismo Beach and San Luis Obispo. There were bad forest fires at the time in Northern California, so I headed back and spent time in San Diego in different neighborhoods, seeing a side of San Diego that I had not experienced before. I visited well over a dozen cities and towns. I would go to Palm Springs for a few days between the travel just to check for mail and do my washing. The repair of the condo took much longer than expected as it was not fully repaired to move back in until early October. After that, I decided that I would sell the condo and move into the penthouse in the same building.

I would say that travel has been one of the passions throughout my life. At age 77, I still have a wish list of places that I would like to see while I still can.

Stanley Papel. Trip Egypt in 2007

Stanley Papel. Trip Laos in 2010

Stanley Papel. Trip Jordan in 2007

Stanley Papel. Trip Cambodia in 2010

Trip Mexico circa 2008, Geri Jacobson (cousin), Stanley Papel, Sophie Papel, Susanna Weinstock (cousin)

Chapter 13

Stanley Papel

FROM BITTERSWEET TO THE GOLDEN YEARS (2016–2019)

An email sent to my family and friends in July 2016:

"Many days, months, and years seem to slip by and meld together and become hard to distinguish as time passes. Yet, there are also important times in our lives that we will always remember.

July 2016 was a month that I will always remember as a "wake up call" to reset the priorities of my life.

On June 30, 2016, I experienced a terrible pain in my stomach that I attributed to food poisoning. However, as the pain continued each night, it became apparent it was something more serious. Soon after, a CT Scan diagnosed diverticulitis, but also unexpected nodular densities and lesions in my liver, lungs and T11 vertebral body that could all be related to each other and malignant. A series of MRI's, scans and lab work followed during the entire month of July, which finally led today to a non-malignant diagnosis by my oncologist. The odds were against these wonderful results.

I am thankful for each day of life and especially for the wonderful family and friends in my life, as well as some of what I was able to achieve in life so far.

I have always been a realist when it comes to life. However, I had not planned to face the possibility of death or cancer treatments at this stage of my life. After the happy diagnosis, I was quickly thankful for 73 happy, healthy years, but I felt a need to prioritize what is really important for the rest of my life going forward, whether it be 1 year, 5 years, or maybe even 30 years—if I have my mom's genes.

If I have already shared some of my journey with you, it is because you were and are part of my support during this most difficult period: my closest family, my dearest friends, my doctors, and even some recent friends who have become an important part of my support during this difficult time.

> *Things that once seemed so important to me are now not important at all. Suddenly, things that were just part of life now are magnified and take on new importance. I am just so thankful for each day and for all the things in my past, present and now future. I realize it is not the quantity of life but rather quality of life. It is not about death...it's about life."*

In July of 2016, my priorities shifted. Family and friends had always been important to me, but they took on even greater meaning when I realized my life may not be as long-lasting as I had hoped. Certainly, my desire to continue my quest for a soul mate dropped from the priority list. More important to me was writing the life story that had been in process for literally twenty-one years. I had started the book project even before coming out. I have gone through coming out, divorcing, a second relationship, weddings, births, deaths, many happy times, some sad times, but this story had not yet been completed.

Coming to terms with death was a big step in my life. I recalled my dad telling me at one time before the Alzheimer's set in (or possibly he knew at the time he was in early stages) that he had a beautiful life and would not change any of it. He asked me only one favor, which was to take care of Mom when something happened to him.

Many years later, Mom told me the same thing about her life. How thankful she was for the wonderful life she had with a wonderful husband, a beautiful family, and having done everything important to her in her life. She said when her time comes, she does not fear death and does not want people to feel sad at her passing but rather to feel happy for her long life. While I was not yet ready to die, I wanted to be thankful for each day and realized the need to put some of the stress behind me and enjoy each day of life. I do have regrets. I have made mistakes in my life that I am sorry about.

My children were all there for me during the month when the future of my life was in question. Melissa accompanied me to every appointment with the oncologist. Evan and Dara were also 100% supportive, and I began to feel a closeness with all three of my children that I hadn't felt before. I wondered why it took a scare like this to bring my family together.

I made a bucket list of what was important in my life going forward and a promise to myself that I needed to put my energies into those priorities. I also thought back to the time in 1981-1982 when I had a series of four eye surgeries and how beautiful the world seemed to me afterwards when I newly appreciated my vision. Yet, as time went by, I took my vision for granted again. This time, it seemed very important to me to not forget that our life spans are brief and to make the most out of our remaining years.

Dropping down on the priority list was my "search" for a partner. I thought, "If it happens, great! However, if I am not partnered again, I have friends and family to be thankful for." Whereas I had made mistakes as a father, I felt that there would still be time to develop a closer bond with my children and also to cherish the grandchildren who were just starting their journey of life.

My career totally dropped from my priority list, and I made a timetable to remove myself from the business. While I would like the business that was started by my dad to continue, it seemed too late for me to make any major difference going forward. If Melissa and Evan could carry on what my dad started, it would be a tribute to him. However, they have their lives and "what will be, will be." Money had always provided me with a sense of security. I realized, however, that from this point forward, I did not need to grow my estate, but rather should enjoy the money I had already earned. I did have an issue with the relatively large debt that I had due to real estate. It became a goal to reduce my liabilities and primarily to live off what I had earned in the past. It was time to enjoy now.

My bucket list emphasized my mental and physical health. My medical health seemed to be what was taken for granted. However, going forward, keeping healthy, both physically and mentally, was essential for my remaining years. Travel had always been a passion. Like many other people my age, I made a list of places I still wanted to visit. I realized though that I really had seen most of the places on earth that were most important to me. I figured that I could still travel for many years, but it was now time to begin seeing the places on this earth that may not be easy to visit as I continue to age.

I also realized that the material possessions were becoming less important to me. It was time to stop acquiring more but rather enjoy what I have already acquired. For years, I had owned two homes: one in West Hollywood since 1996; and the other in Palm Springs also since 1996. I thought for the first time that I would not always be able to maintain two homes. At some point, I would need to choose between Palm Springs and Los Angeles. Like my mom and dad, as they aged, they returned to their base, which was Los Angeles. I was not ready to make any changes yet, but downsizing became a goal.

By the end of July 2016 I got the "all clear." The growths that had been discovered within my body were found to be non-malignant. The oncologist told me it is seldom the case when he sees something like what was showing up on the initial scans that he can give "good news." The message to me was that my time on this planet is not yet complete. Would I take this good news and work on my life to make others and myself happier going forward? I hoped so. The control would be in my hands, and it would be up to me as to what I would do with this second lease on life.

In August 2016 I made a long planned trip to England and Germany. I have to say that I saw Europe differently from past trips. I usually take the Underground (the Tube) from Heathrow Airport to the stop in Earl's Court near my hotel. I was still feeling very lucky to be alive, and was able to be more spontaneous on this trip and just enjoy each day as it unfolded. I hadn't been to Berlin or Munich for several years, and I started to think that this could be my last trip to these places.

I was turning 74 on December 17th and scheduled a family get-together where all the kids, spouses and grandkids were invited to spend time in Carlsbad and San Diego. It was a very happy time because we were all close, and I was still feeling so lucky to be alive.

My parents loved to travel. In their later travel years, they cruised primarily on Crystal Cruises. They said Crystal is the absolute best and that I should experience that level of luxury travel. So, I booked a 7-day cruise off the coast off California visiting places I have been to many times. However, the enjoyment would be not specifically where I visited as much as just enjoying the comfort level of the cruise. I'd like to take another Crystal cruise again, but there are still so many places that I would like to visit while I am still active.

The other strong recommendation that my parents made was to take a trip to the Canadian Rockies. They said it was much more beautiful than the American Rockies and said that Banff,

Lake Louise, and Jasper National Park should all be on my wish list. Since there were many destinations involved, I decided to take a group tour that provided all the transportation between the destinations. It included Fairmont Hotels and nearly all meals. I figured that I had worked hard all my life and now it was time to enjoy some luxuries.

I started the trip by flying first to Toronto to visit my good friend Alex Waugh. From Toronto, I flew to Calgary where I met the group of 40 travelers and where the tour began. All were married except for two single ladies and myself. It was a friendly group, but I mostly paired off with the single ladies. One the of the ladies, Robin Lesser, became a very good friend, and since then we have traveled together as well as my hosting her at my home during her visits to Palm Springs.

Something else happened on this trip which was life changing. On August 25, 2017, I went online out of curiosity to see what single gay men were available in Calgary. There was a good-looking man by the name of Sven Wulf who had contacted me and said he wanted to meet me. I explained that I was on a group tour and this wasn't really the type of trip where I was looking to date. I had wanted to stick with the group, which seemed to be on the go 24/7. Sven did not want to take "no" for an answer. However, we did Skype on that trip and started to keep in touch regularly.

On October 6, 2017, Sven flew from Calgary for a visit with me in Los Angeles. We spent the next six days together, and it felt very comfortable for both of us. We did start to date. However, there were a lot of complications because Sven lived and worked in Canada, and I did not want a "long distance" relationship. Still, we did keep in regular contact, and in November 2017 we drove together from Calgary to Los Angeles with stops along the way in Montana, Idaho, Utah, Nevada and then on to Los Angeles. Sven then stayed with me in Los Angeles and Palm Springs until January 2018 when he returned to Canada to try to work things through as to whether we would be able to live together as partners. It was a bumpy year in 2018 because I knew that I wanted to be with Sven but Sven was in Canada. Then, on August 31, 2018, Sven visited me in San Diego while I was still on my "Vagabond" trip. We made a mutual decision on that day that we were going to be together. Sven was not "out," and part of the difficulty for Sven was to come out as a gay man to his family and friends.

Everything moved very quickly after the decision was made that Sven and I would become partners. Soon we met with an immigration attorney who recommended that if we eventually planned on marrying, then we should do so soon rather than wait because Sven's status of entering on a tourist visa was in question due to his many entries into the USA. We decided on a small wedding of just a very few close friends and family, which happened on December 1, 2018. At that time, we also decided on having a larger reception with all family and close friends that would be a "Marriage Celebration" at a beautiful restaurant called La Bohème in West Hollywood. The event took place on September 23, 2019, after nine months of much happiness together.

For years I had wondered, "when do I end this story?" Life goes on, and there are always new and important parts of life to include. For example, we just recently had the happy news that my daughter, Dara, will be marrying Todd Weinger in May 2020. They are a beautiful couple, and it is with such pleasure than I know my three children are all in happy unions.

Father's Day 2008

3 Generations. Joe, Evan and Stanley Papel in 2014

Phinley Papel's Bris in 2011

Family Vacation. San Diego in 2016

Grandchildren. Phinley Papel, Lily Moscot, Oliver Moscot, Joe Papel in 2017

Stanley Papel and Sven Wulf. Wedding December 1, 2018

Children of Stanley Papel and their Spouses (left to right):
Todd and Dara Weinger, Evan and Debbi Papel, Melissa and Gregg Moscot in 2019

Stanley Papel and Sven Wulf. Roadtrip Pacific Coast 2019

Stanley Papel and Sven Wulf. Marriage Celebration September 21, 2019

Stanley Papel and Sven Wulf. Marriage Celebration September 21, 2019 ...
Bernie Kamens, Stanley Papel, Sophie Papel, Sven Wulf

CHAPTER 14

STANLEY PAPEL
STRANGER THAN LIFE

There are a few events in my life that are difficult to explain. I consider myself a realist and have not believed in the afterlife or spiritual connections from the non-living. However, several things have happened to me that seemed stranger than life.

In 2011, a hand-carved wooden statue of a kneeling Buddhist disciple was given to me by my cousin, Geoffrey Bellah. The statue had belonged to Geoffrey's mentor and close friend, Robert Lawrence Balzer, a well-known wine journalist who had converted to Buddhism as a young man. Nearing the end of his life, Robert gave Geoffrey many of his cherished possessions, including this large beautifully hand-carved statue from Cambodia. Unfortunately for Geoffrey, he had no place in his home for the statue, and he asked me if I wanted it. Having been to Cambodia and returning without any mementos, I thought it would be a good connection.

After having the statue in my home for several months, I was sitting on the couch drinking a glass of wine one evening. All of a sudden, out of nowhere, a force came out of the statue. It looked around the living room and then at me. I was scared. As the force roamed around the house, I had the feeling that it was saying, "It is okay. The statue is fine here. I will not come back but the statue belongs here."

I tried to phone Geoffrey the next morning to tell him of this odd experience but could not reach him. Instead, I sent Geoffrey an email telling him of the incident and asked about Robert. He responded that Robert had passed away that same evening of December 2, 2011, just shortly before I had the "visit." It seemed so real and beyond coincidence. So, I believe now that there is some type of spiritual force.

Another event that has left me baffled relates to a now good friend, Phil Rrig, who rented my guest house in Palm Springs shortly after it was built in 2015. He is from the Yap Islands, a small country in the South Pacific located between the Philippines and Guam. When he moved into the guest house, he told me about his only relationship with a man by the name of Blake who had suddenly passed away. They lived together in Hawaii. Blake was an attorney for the government and often traveled to the different territories in the South Pacific where the United States has special interests. Blake's death happened so quickly that Phil and Blake didn't even have a chance to say, "goodbye." They were both in their early 40's at the time this happened.

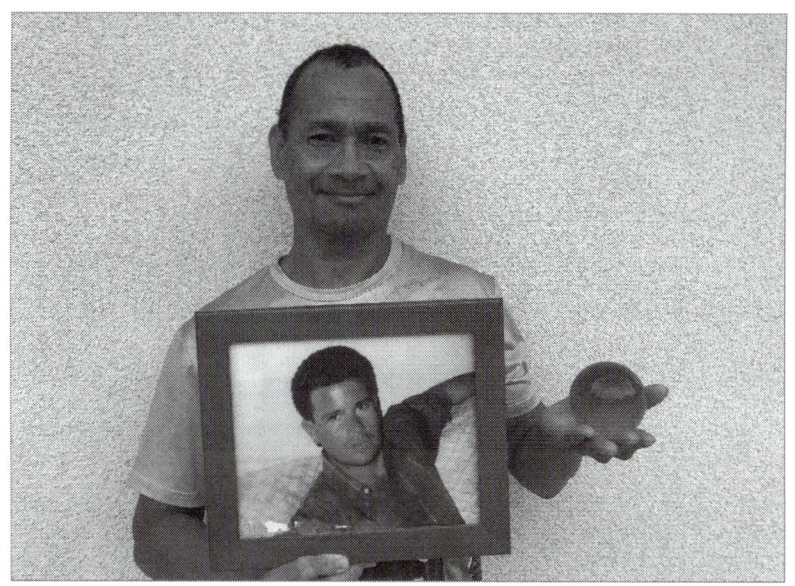

Phil Rrig with photo of Blake Philips

It's hard to put into words, but I somehow felt like Blake wanted to connect with Phil through me. Phil had told me that Blake called him his "golden crystal" which referred to his Pacific Islander skin color and being a special person in his life. In any event, I was in San Francisco and felt like I wanted to pick up a little gift for Phil and thought of maybe purchasing a "golden crystal." I was at Fisherman's Wharf and didn't see anything, so I planned to just head back on my normal long walk down Mason Street, which takes me directly in front of my owned timeshare at The Donatello on Post and Mason in San Francisco.

As I was walking back, something made me turn and go out of my way through Chinatown. Normally, I would never deviate from my route back to the hotel. Still, when I reached Chinatown, I was somehow drawn into this little Chinese shop, where I immediately saw a golden crystal ball on a stand. It was priced higher than I would normally spend on a friend for whom I just wanted to buy a little trinket. Still, I bought it and gave it to Phil when I returned from San Francisco. His eyes teared up, and he told me that was the same exact piece that Blake had given to Phil as a gift. After Blake's death, Blake's brother came to Hawaii and had removed all of the items that he thought belonged to Blake, including the golden crystal that had been gifted to Phil. I told Phil that I think Blake momentarily lived on through me and that this was his way of communicating with him, and to let Phil know that he needed the closure to tell Phil goodbye and that he loved him.

It's just too strange when something like this happens. It seems beyond coincidence. I will never know why something like this happens. I am left wondering if this was pure coincidence or if it is something beyond.

Great Grandfather Louis Fisch.
"I am not a gambler and a drunk".
Refer to preface

CHAPTER 15

STANLEY PAPEL
REFLECTIONS

The manuscript for my life story was begun in April 1995. The story continued until September 2019 with the marriage celebration of Sven and me. Today, it is April 1, 2020, and the manuscript is now complete with the exception of this brief epilogue.

As I write this, we find ourselves experiencing some very strange times in the world today—times that will certainly go down in history. We don't currently have the benefit of knowing what will happen next. We only know that we are in the early stages of battling the Coronavirus, known as COVID-19, which began in China in January 2020.

In our home state of California, we have been under a "shelter in place" order since March 20, 2020. All non-essential businesses have been closed through April, and we are asked to remain at home and socially distance ourselves from others so as to not acquire or spread the disease. Presently, over 75% of the USA population is now under "shelter in place" orders. It is a very different world today than it was only a month ago. No one knows how intense the death rate will excel until there is a vaccination in place. Currently, confirmed cases in the world are about 1,000,000. Death rate so far is 60,000. No one knows at this point in time how many people will die from the coronavirus before a vaccine is developed.

Once busy schedules for most people have dwindled to become largely free time except for those who are able to work from home. The world is definitely in a major transition, and even once the virus is under control, there will likely be many significant changes to our way of life.

For me, this time at home has offered me additional time for completing and re-editing the book's manuscript in order to finalize the draft for publishing. However, even more important, this has given me additional quiet time to reflect on my life. I think about life decisions that proved to be right, along with those which proved to be wrong. I think about what I want to do differently with the rest of my life, no matter how short or long that will be. We have already lost a friend to the Coronavirus, and I don't know how many more people I know personally will die from this pandemic. It emphasizes the fragility and uncertainty of life.

As I was editing one of the more difficult chapters in this book, a song was playing in the background called "My Way," written by Paul Anka. The song became an anthem for his friend, Frank Sinatra, one of the twentieth century's most popular entertainers.

For those not familiar with the lyrics, they tell about a man who has lived a full life and chose to live it "his way." There were times when he made mistakes, and at other times, he may have tried to take on more than he could handle. Even so, he lived his life the way he chose, without compromise. I related very much to that song because it is the same way that I made decisions affecting my life. I do have regrets. There are things that I would have done differently if I had the option of reliving my life. There is no need to run through my regrets at this point as they are mentioned elsewhere in this book. However, ultimately, I take responsibly for my own decisions, for the good ones I have made, and for my mistakes as well.

As I write this epilogue the world is in a stage of uncertainty beyond what I have experienced in my lifetime. At 77 years old, I look back on my life and reflect. I hope I have many more years ahead of me yet. However, life will end for everyone at some point. I am so thankful for my life and to the wonderful parents who raised me. I am also thankful for bringing life into this world and hope there will be generations after me who can learn from their parents and from the family and friends who helped shape their lives.

Life is beautiful and I am blessed with a lifetime of wonderful friends and family.

So ends this portion of the book on my life. I would be extremely honored if you would take the time to read about the lives of my parents, grandparents, and other members of our family.

L'chaim…To Life!

MAJOR EVENTS IN THE LIFE OF STANLEY PAPEL

1942 — Birth of Stanley Papel

1943 — Lived with Mom and Grandparents (Roth) on Third Avenue in Los Angeles

1945 — End of World War II

1946 — Moved to first home located on Butler Avenue in West Los Angeles

1947 — Birth of sister, Arlene Papel

1954 — Moved with parents to "dream home" on Cashmere Terrace, Brentwood, Los Angeles, CA

1955 — Bar Mitzvah

1955 — First Ruggles Gift Shop opened in Disneyland, Anaheim, CA

1960 — Graduation University High School. Started college at UCLA

1964 — Graduation from UCLA with Bachelor of Arts in Psychology

1965 — Started first career position at Bank of America, Los Angeles, CA

1967 — Graduated from UCLA with Master of Business Administration in Consumer Behavior.

1967 — Three months of travel to Europe and Mediterranean

1967 — Started second career position at May Department Stores, Los Angeles, CA

1970 — Started career position at Ruggles Gifts and Papel Imports (47 years)

1972 — Married Aileen Miller

1974 — Birth of daughter, Melissa Papel

1975 — Moved to first owned home as married couple on Kearsarge St. in Brentwood, LA

1976 — Birth of son, Evan Papel

1977 — Moved to "dream home" on Weddington Street in Encino, CA

1981 — Four eye surgeries for retinal detachment (1981–1982)

1982 — Papel Giftware obtains 1984 Olympic Games license in Los Angeles

1986 — Birth of daughter, Darrah (Dara) Papel

1987 — Papel Giftware is sold to RUSS (Russ Berrie & Co.)

1990 — Employment with RUSS terminates. Career continues in Licensing as Papel Designs

1995 — Trip to Nepal. Began writing Life Story and coming to terms with my life

1995 — Came out as a gay (bisexual) man. Legal separation with Aileen

1996 — Moved to first owned home as a single man on Alfred St. in West Hollywood, CA

1997 — Bought first home in Palm Springs, CA on Calle Rolph

1998 — Divorce finalized with Aileen. Became domestic partners with Kent Chamberlin.

1998 — Death of Father, Phil Papel. Mother, Sophie Papel turns 80

2000 — Started import business of socks under name of Papel Designs in Palm Springs, CA

2004 — Marriage of daughter, Melissa Papel to Gregg Moscot

2006 — Separation and dissolution of partnership with Kent Chamberlin

2007 — Birth of first granddaughter, Lily Moscot to Melissa and Gregg Moscot

2011 — Birth of first grandson, Oliver Moscot, to Melissa and Gregg Moscot

2012 — Marriage of son, Evan Papel to Deborah Roseman

2012 — Sold home on Alfred Street in West Hollywood

2012 — Bought primary home on Pinto Road in Palm Springs, CA

2014 — Birth of second grandson, Joe Papel, to Evan and Debbi Papel

2016 — Cancer Scare (turned out benign)

2016 — Birth of third grandson, Phinley Papel to Evan and Debbi Papel

2018 — Retired from Papel Designs

2018 — Sophie Papel turns 100

2018 — Marriage of Stanley Papel to Sven Wulf

2019 — Completed the draft edition of *Tales Beyond Main Street* (Story of Papel Giftware)

2020 — Marriage of daughter, Dara Papel to Todd Weiner

2020 — Finished writing this book after 25 years

2020 — Birth of fifth grandchild, Shane Meyer Papel to Evan and Debbi Papel

PART II
Phil Papel
(1916–1998)

ANCESTRY CHART
FOR
PHILIP PAPEL

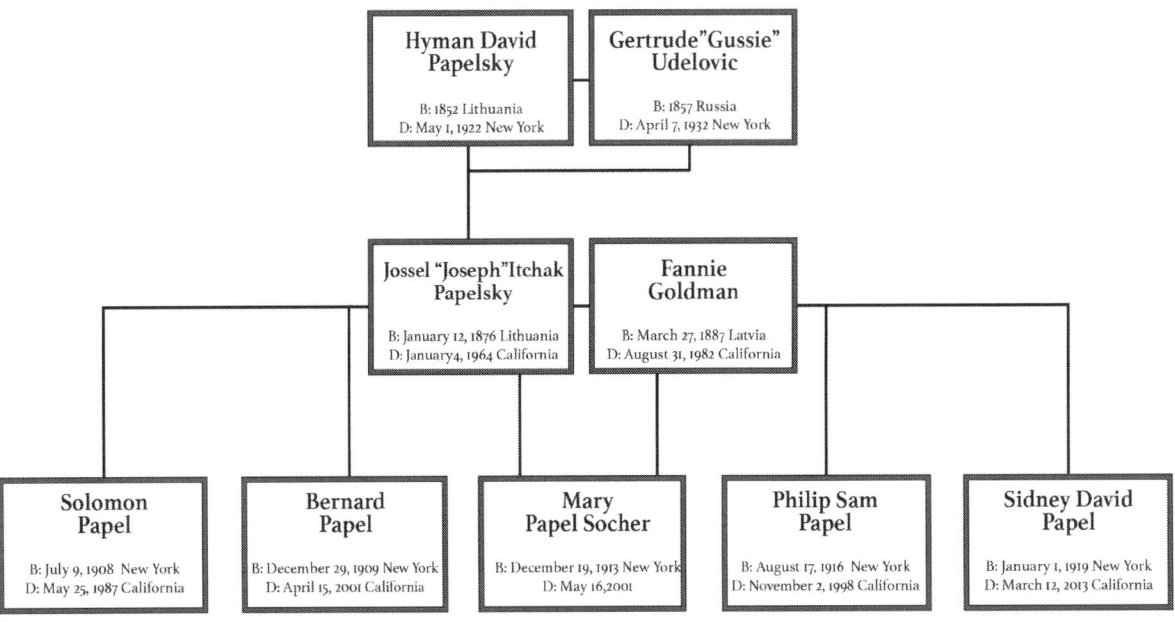

Life Story of Phil Papel

By Phil Papel

For several years, my sweet and loving daughter, Arlene, has been asking me to write the story of my life. I have procrastinated, whether from laziness or my questioning, whether I am qualified to hold anyone's interest with a prolonged story of my life. In all frankness, I seriously doubt that anyone other than my family and close friends would enjoy having some recorded background of my childhood days and a knowledge of the series of events in the course of my lifetime that until now have contributed to my good fortune.

At this moment, Sophie and I are vacationing in New Zealand at a hotel located at the base of the Franz Josef Glazier. History will record that on this date and the three days preceding it, the very heaviest rainfall recorded in this area isolated us from the world. Radio contact has been lost and bridges on both sides of the community have been washed away. There is one airstrip with three or four small planes that remain in good shape, and because of that, the approximately 600 people here are in good spirits with no fear of any genuine danger. We have been advised of having possibly three to five days to relax and enjoy ourselves. With that much time provided, God has made it clear to me that I should start the story of my life.

I was born in Brooklyn, New York, on August 17, 1916. While there are things that I recall about my childhood days, I do not consider the early days of my life to be all that exciting and interesting.

My parents worked very hard to keep our family of five children fed and clothed. We were poor, but certainly not without life's necessities. While my dad, Joseph Papel (aka Popilsky), worked long hours and had little to enjoy the pleasures of family life, he was a contented and kind person. I could never recall him punishing any of us children for things we were not supposed to do.

Our loving mother was the "captain" of our ship and directed all of us, mildly punishing us when we deserved it and ensuring that all of our needs were supplied while handling the finances. She earned any extra dollar she could, whether it be helping a neighborhood grocer or cleaning. Fannie was always there with a smile on her face and a song in her heart.

When I was approximately six years old, my sister, Mary, developed a rheumatic heart problem and the doctor suggested moving to California. The California dry climate, he felt, would give her the opportunity to live a normal life. With no money, but plenty of spirit and courage, the decision was made. My mother took all the children to sunny California. My father joined us several months later. Fortunately, most of mother's brothers and sisters were already here, and the children lived with different members of the family until my father arrived.

I remember our first residence was at 1207 North Evergreen in Los Angeles. I started school at Malabar Street Elementary and did not give anyone a difficult time except for my mother. I had strange consumption habits, eating very little. It bothered her that I did not eat her good solid foods such as chicken matzo ball soup and brisket. Incidentally, I remained thin all through my early years—at the time of my marriage, when I was almost 23 and 6'-1/2" tall, I weighed only 149 pounds.

My business career started when I was in the 3rd grade. There was a paper route for the Los Angeles Evening Herald servicing the area around Wabash and Evergreen. I helped the delivery boy fold the papers each day and was paid two cents. The corner was also a meeting area for other kids my age. While folding papers one day, I was engaged by a kind elderly man in a conversation. I told him that often someone wanted me to buy a paper route. He stated that he was the district manager and offered me a job selling papers at that spot. At least six to eight other people had heard about it and they all wanted to do it, but I was the lucky one he selected. I started the first day with ten papers and continued selling there until I graduated high school. I sold more than 200 papers at that time and got to know almost everyone in Boyle Heights.

My junior high and high school days were happy ones as I enjoyed school, but I always had to rush directly from class to get to my "corner" as quickly as I could. We had moved to City Terrace, well over a mile from my "corner," and I would usually arrive home after most of the family had eaten dinner. I would drop all of my money into my mother's lap, just as everyone else in the family did. We all did our share of helping the family, and Mom never complained about anyone being lazy. Apparently, we all felt a responsibility and were willing to do our part ungrudgingly.

My brother Sol was the most successful. At a time when radios were being bought by most families, he was an excellent repair man and had all the work he could handle. Sol's philosophy was also to "live it up" and he possibly could have saved more money than he did, at least that is what I heard. Mom criticized him often for his spending habits and I believe she was right.

My relationship with my brothers and sister was good. Sol was the only one that physically would take it upon himself to "teach me a lesson" and I remember thinking that I would get even with him later in life when I would be up in years, but of course he would be older as well. I would try to pin him down, but I ultimately gave up, for he was also the one that took me to ball games, auto races, and bought me delicious ten-cent Chapman's ice cream cones. I always felt that in time of need, he would really be there for me. Thankfully, there was no such time that developed during the years ahead.

My sister, Mary, was a good soul that gave no one any problems. Looking back, I think we could have been great friends, but our choice of friends and mates just made it impossible.

Bernie (Bernard) was a lover of fine music, but a frustrated soul that had no talent as a self-taught clarinet player. Odd in his own way, he would not hurt a fly. I hate for my life story to be told and include bitterness, but it is certainly there. He married a woman that had problems in her lifetime that she simply could not cope with. Ethyl successfully changed Bernie from someone who was close to his mother and dad to someone concerned solely with his own success, the dollar, and Ethyl. While the book remains open to the wisdom of life's pattern, he chose to deny his parents the love and affection that they so badly wanted from him. My own opinion of him and his chosen mate is such that it is best not put any more about him into writing.

Sidney is the one I have been closest to; we have been and always will have a relationship of trust, confidence, and brotherly love.

If I were to tell a more complete story of my life, I must revert to my high school days before my graduation in the summer of 1933. Without telling me, my mother regularly deposited some or all of my newspaper earnings in the U.S. National Bank for continuing my education. My high

Phil Papel. Roosevelt High School Graduation Los Angeles, CA circa 1934

school biology teacher, Mr. Griffith, developed an interest in me and encouraged me to become an Osteopath (like a M.D.). I had hopes of entering the College of Osteopathy, which was then located directly across the street from our general hospital. Unfortunately, the bank closed that spring and there was no federal insurance at the time. Sidney took over my newspaper corner, and I went looking for a job, finally holding a series of brief jobs. I was 16 at the time and worked as a warehouseman at Sears Roebuck ($16.00 a week), sold day-old cakes at the Grand Central Market ($12.00 a week), a warehouseman in a ladies undergarment factory, plus six months building fire breaks and planting trees in the Civilian Conservation Corps (C.C.C.) at $30.00 a month. Somewhere in between all of this, I continued my schooling with a semester at L.A. City College. I had a nighttime position washing dishes at Carpenter's Drive-In located at Sunset and Vine (Hollywood). It paid $2 a night plus meals with hours of 11 p.m. to 7 a.m. It was conveniently close to school (L.A.C.C.) and the usual daily routine was class from 8 a.m. to 2-3 p.m., home to get some sleep and do homework and on the job at 11 p.m.

*Phil Papel. CCC Camp
(Civilian Conservation Corp.)
Los Angeles, CA in 1935*

I really did not do that well at school, missing two finals while sleeping on the lawn. However, I gained tremendous experience as a polished dishwasher, drying with two towels at once; all of which came in handy in later years as I entered marriage.

Except for my time at C.C.C.'s, I regularly attended night school taking a variety of subjects, including a civil service class. The purpose of the class was to prepare me for examinations. However, I was only 17 years old and had not thought of brushing up my education with a course that was really a general review of everything we were supposed to have learned in high school.

Near the end of the summer session, the instructor asked for a show of hands to determine which students had applied for the postal clerk and carrier examinations about to be held. The final day for registering was approaching. I did not raise my hand, and the instructor apparently noted it. He asked that I see him after class, inquired what type of work I had been doing and recommended that I take the examination. My reply was that I thought I was too young (I had just turned 18). Wrong! All I had to be was 18. I passed with a 96.7 percent.

I had a choice of locations where I was to start as a substitute, garnering 65 cents per house as the youngest mail carrier in Los Angeles. I chose good old Boyle Heights, the area where I grew up and felt so much at ease. I was the envy of my friends for my earnings average of $30-

*Phil Papel.
Catalina Island in 1936*

$35 a week, a sum that seemed tremendous. Before very long, a regular district became available and I had my own district #141 with a salary of $1600 per year, advancing each year $100 until the top salary of $2100 could be achieved. During the years ahead, I continued my limited schooling with night classes at UCLA Extension.

My social life was becoming more interesting as I naturally did some dating but did not find a special person that held my attraction. On a Saturday night, June 27, 1936, a close friend called to ask my plans for the evening. We discussed every possibility including the casino in Ocean Park, trying to get enough fellows for a poker game, a show, and whatever. Nothing worked out.

I finally remembered a party that I had been invited to, which I had previously declined, at the home of my ex-boss from the garment factory. He had three daughters, pleasant enough, but the mother was totally impossible without going into details. She clearly wanted me in the family and I wanted no part of it. However, with nothing else to do and after explaining to my friend all the details, it was agreed we would go and leave when we desired. I called the hostess to tell some story advising of the change in plans and asked for permission to bring my friend.

I was asked to pick up a girl who needed transportation to the party. Of course, I agreed to do it although that girl was definitely not my date for the evening. It was at that party that I met Sophie Roth and was immediately attracted to her. The only problem was that my friend appeared to be interested in her as well. Before I could ask to bring her home, he did. I drove home with the same girl we had originally picked up in the front seat while my friend sat in the rear with Sophie. You can be sure I found many things to talk about to keep my friend busy conversing openly.

At any rate, I remembered Sophie's house and shortly thereafter called on her for the first date. I do not believe it is necessary to reveal details of our long courtship. That first date, other than my birthday, was the most important day of my life. Nothing of what lies ahead could have been accomplished if her love, confidence, and trust had not been there. She was involved in making of every significant move in addition to being an inspiration. She has always been there to involve herself with good advice and the sincere deep desire to help in any fashion. If

*Phil Papel and Sophie Roth.
Catalina Island in 1938*

*Phil Papel and Sophie Roth.
Catalina Island in 1938*

there is to be a dedication of this story of my life, certainly it would be to her.

At any rate, in courting Sophie, I felt I needed a new car and so I bought a 1937 Dodge with a two-year contract paying $35.63 monthly.

For that period, I knew Sophie was the "love of my life" but I could not save enough money to even consider marriage. The car was finally fully paid for in early 1939. The marriage date was set for May 21st of that year. Since that time, I have never bought a car unless I could pay cash.

We went through all the financial problems most young people did during that period. There was very little furniture to start with in a single apartment at $32.00 per month. I was doing fairly well for the times, but always had just enough funds to pay our bills. Buying a single piece of furniture was a big event. Restaurant dinners were reserved for only special occasions, our principle treat being a Sunday morning brunch for 39 cents consisting of orange juice, bacon, eggs, waffles and coffee.

If all this sounds like we were struggling and unhappy, believe me, such was not the case. We were extremely happy, but we just wanted a bit more.

So, I did keep taking an interest in a better paying position within the civil service. I had passed the Border Patrol Inspector's examination and was called in but failed the physical. The job called for 20/20 vision without glasses. Not getting the job did not bother me after I learned what the demands of the job were. I also passed the examination for Railway Mail Clerk, a position that started at the salary paid to carriers after five years, and also advanced

Phil and Sophie Papel. Wedding May 21, 1939

each year for five years at $100 per year. This job was a new position that I did want. I resigned my position as carrier.

My seniority at my new job was low. As a result, my hours and days were not the best. For a very long two years, my workday started with a 3:30 AM alarm. Sophie would awake along with me, prepare a breakfast in spite of me not wanting her to, and I drove to the Lockheed Air Terminal in Burbank for the 5 a.m. shift. I would be home early afternoon, study my "schemes" and still have plenty of time for us to have a reasonable social life. I really enjoyed the challenge of the new job. Certainly, it was far more interesting and, as one would expect, each month's work was far easier than the month before.

On December 7th, 1941, I recall the excitement at the airmail field when details of Pearl Harbor became known. The period ahead affected everyone, and there was great confusion as to just how the war going to affect the county and each of us as individuals. Sophie and I had moved into a larger apartment with the expectations of starting our family. I had no knowledge of my position in the military draft as there seemed to be a general belief that the importance of the efficiency of certain key areas of the postal system would exempt those working at the airmail field.

We went ahead with our family plans, and one year and 10 days after Pearl Harbor, December 17, 1942, Stanley Louis Papel was born. Sophie had a very difficult time as she was in labor for more than 14 hours. As usual, Stan was thinking about it and had not quite made up his mind as to when he was to make his appearance. When he did, we were thrilled with what we had as the new addition to our family, and we became even more so as the time went on.

I did not enjoy for long the early parts of Stan's childhood as Uncle Sam pointed his finger right at me and firmly, but politely said, "Please come. We camp in San Diego." All bills were paid and there was $50 in the bank. I kept $25 and left Sophie with $25, returning my wife to her parents with a beautiful new baby and selected pieces of furniture we did not want to part with.

My experiences in boot camp were typical of those hundreds of thousands that went into the service. None of us knew just what was ahead, but none of us appeared to be worried. Certainly, it was not a soft program. It was designed to teach us authority and to get us all in good physical shape. The program certainly did all of that plus some pleasures in the form of night movies and entertainment provided by many well-known professionals who dedicated their time and energies for that purpose.

I took advantage of that diversion a few times before realizing that I could make some extra money in the evenings by washing leggings for many of the men in our company who were willing to pay 50 cents a pair to have it done. It was not too difficult a job, and I was able to save a small sum of money that I might use for my boot camp leave after six weeks of training. Six weeks went by fast and then that time did elapse. I, along with the rest of the company, headed to the Exchange with (the) purpose of buying a traveling bag for our leave home before (receiving) our transfer orders. None were available as they had just sold out. All we could use was a small white canvas bag that they provided, which was just barely large enough to hold a change of underwear and a toothbrush.

The training station was divided into a series of camps. The "boots" were in Camp Decatur. On the other side of the station was another camp where those who had returned from leave were stationed awaiting processing for transfer. I figured that they must be returning with bags they would not have any use for and (would be) impossible to keep. So, history was made. I took the bus that circled the station finally ending up at the returning area. I was right. I discovered that all kinds of bags were available, some beautiful, others with torn zippers, etc. But they were of absolutely no use to the man about to be shipped out. I bought an armload, averaging about a dollar a bag and sold them to the eager buyers in my company for about double my cost. With all the extra money that I now had, I was able to buy my new son a plaything, Sophie a pin, and each of the mothers a gift. I went home for what I then thought would be my last homecoming for a long time and I treasured every moment. The time went fast, and then I was back to camp, receiving overseas shots, and awaiting notice of transfer to places unknown.

About the second or third day after my return, I received notice to meet with an officer for reasons not stated. I was the only one in the company singled out for the instructions, and I was more than curious. My records had revealed my postal background, and they needed someone with the same experience to be in charge of the post office within the area. I had just had my training, Camp Decatur. Could I handle it? I was positive I could. It was a perfect arrangement for me as the responsibility was one easily handled. They gave me quarters that were ideal, time to continue to see my family, plus the ability to continue the "bag" business in the evenings.

For the first few weeks, I bought bags one evening, repaired and cleaned them, and the following night sold them. Operating the post office was absolutely no problem, and I received words of commendation from the officer in charge of all the camp's post offices. The demand for bags remained heavy; the problem was getting enough of them and the time consumed in both getting them and repairing those that needed it. Nonetheless, it was a great business, and I earned on average $150 a week, all of it going into the bank. I was able to arrange schedules and had the privilege of parking my car on base. I would drive home each Friday evening with a full load of my friends and return to camp on Sunday. This was during the period when cars driving that route were permitted to use their dimmer lights only, referred to as a "blackout."

One beautiful Saturday afternoon I decided to take Stan for a ride in his Taylor Tot. There was a Western Auto Supply store close by and on display was a beautiful leather trimmed collapsible waterproof bag reduced to $1.50. Prices were controlled during that period, and all the original prices were posted. They could be reduced, but not increased. The original price was $5.00. My mind churned. If I could concentrate my time selling only, without buying and repairing, I believed I could possibly double my earnings. I asked the manager the extent of his inventory. My car trunk would hold exactly 16 dozen bags, and after paying him, I asked him to obtain another 16 dozen for the week to follow. By that time, the post exchange received their supply of bags, but my bag at $3.00 was far superior to the one they offered in the same price range. I also went into each of the barracks as the "boots" came into the area designated for leave and their "shopping" was made easy. I did, in fact, double my earnings and legitimately make more money than the captain of the station. That money went directly into the bank. While all good things must come to an end, it was that money earned in the four months of "Papel's Bags" that financed my venture into the gift business.

The end came some four months later when I got sick while on leave. I developed strep throat and checked into the Long Beach Naval Hospital for treatment. My records were automatically transferred to the 11th Naval District for further transfer. A week or 10 days later, I was given a short leave awaiting papers for my overseas assignment that I was certain to receive within three days. It did. To my surprise a post office was to be set up on San Clemente Island and I was to be responsible for its design and operation.

The 31st Division of the Naval Construction Battalion (Cee Bees; aka Navy Seabees) was stationed there. An airfield operated with full maintenance navy personnel and both marines and army companies trained there for short periods.

On my arrival, I discussed and designed rough plans for the office to be used with the Cee Bees. I was astounded as within three or four days we were open and in business. Always in a fog belt, it was hard to believe it was desirable as an airship base. There was no fresh water and not too much to look at.

There were many advantages. I could get home fairly regularly on leave. I was totally in charge and while not a dietician, I did believe we should have fresh fruit regularly in our

Phil and Sophie Papel.
You're in the Navy now circa 1943

working area; particularly as the cooks and bakers worked during mail call hours and deserved special means of getting their mail. They did appreciate my recognition of their problem and cooperated when our mail specialties (that was our rating) had to work on weekends and would want to have a few steaks, solid tomatoes, a ride out to a secluded spot on the island to have our own private barbeque. Living as we did, there were many incidents. I can recall some that were really quite funny, some sad, but in all sincerity, I felt we were doing a good job in getting mail from home to men that were anxiously awaiting their arrival.

Shortly before the war ended, I had an experience that ended my naval career. I was about to leave for a weekend at home, which usually meant riding a destroyer into San Diego, then taking a train into Los Angeles, an all-day procedure, when I was asked if I wanted to fly into Port Hueneme aboard a Douglas SBD Dauntless—a 20 minute flight. The two-seater plane was a Navy bomber that had made an emergency landing on the island. It had been repaired and the pilot was all set to take off. I had no time for a life belt or chute. Without hesitation, I jumped into the plane and we were off. As we approached the mainland, I could see a bit of fog, but I felt certain that would be no problem. But as we were apparently preparing for a landing, I could see we were in trouble with signs he could not lower his landing wheels. For possibly less, but what seemed like an hour, he would dive the craft and would suddenly snap it into a sharp climb hoping the wheels would shake lose. My problem was that my stomach was still going down. Many maneuvers involved proceeding on a straight path, suddenly shooting up and then down or the reverse, down, and then up again. It was an experience. While all this was going on, the fog was becoming thicker and thicker. The pilot then indicated to me that he wanted me to jump. I had no chute and while I know he understood, I feared that he might just choose to jump anyway. As I write it now, it seems almost like a comedy, but at the time, it was anything but that. I actually thought the end was near.

The field at Hueneme was surrounded by high Eucalyptus trees and I saw that we had just cleared the tops and were in fact coming for a landing, but across the landing strips with wheels up. It was also clear they the field controllers knew we were in trouble as there was all kinds of fire equipment rushing to us as we touched down, flipped to what seemed like a 90-degree angle and came down right side up. I had braced the front of the cockpit in front of me, and the jolt which quickly followed was okay. Within seconds, we were surrounded by the fire-fighting men and powerful hoses. I was in perfect condition, went home and never said a word to Sophie about it until months later. I was certain if she knew she would not want me flying again.

Following the incident, I returned to duty, and it developed into quite a story at our air station. Most thought he (the pilot) was incompetent. He had been there for several weeks waiting to repair the plane. I would have no way of knowing, but I was told that he could have physically cranked the wheels down. At any rate, he did not jump and he did get us in safely, so wherever he is today, he still has my deep appreciation. I do owe him a most grateful thanks.

That same week, because of my involvement in the crash, I was advised that I was to check into our infirmary for a checkup. They found my blood pressure was extremely high. It was the only thing that was apparently wrong with me, and while the doctor was concerned, he attributed it to all the excitement I had been through and requested I continually come back, which I did for two months. He gave me no medication, but apparently they did not have it to give. Finally, the doctor felt I should be transferred to the Long Beach Naval Hospital for observation. I cannot recall a more boring period of my life. I felt good but was not permitted to even help sort mail. I just ate and rested for six weeks. I could walk outdoors and visit with those that came to visit, but every few hours, I had to take my (blood) pressure and at least two or three times a night they would wake me up and strap a belt around my arm for another reading.

The doctors were pleasant, but some were blunt and didn't care for my feelings. One young doctor—apparently fresh out of school—made the remark that "I was like a time bomb ready to explode. I would not live to be 35." I did not appreciate it and let him know it. Finally, after my long vacation, I appeared before a medical board and received an honorable discharge.

Another interesting chapter of my life was about to begin. The only direction that I was certain of was my strong desire never to return to the post office again. My seniority, which I was about to lose, was seven years of service plus my time in the Navy. However, I felt that I had no future and that the challenges ahead were not sufficiently rewarding. I was willing to gamble, as I believed I could do better and Sophie agreed. I literally had no experience in business and fielded no offers. I did have several suggestions and conversations, but they were meaningless. After a very short period of confusion, I made a big decision. I would return to school and become a medical doctor. I checked all my credits and enrolled at USC to complete my pre-med requirements, which could be done in one year. Then it would take me four years to graduate.

Additionally, I would have to complete a one-year internship and one final year of residency. A long time considering that I was in my late 20's (an old man). Thankfully, financially, I would be greatly helped by my G.I. Bill.

I visited my mother on the Friday proceeding the Monday that I was set to start my new career. She was to learn the "big" decision. Directly in front of where she resided, a young couple rented a shop about the size of a garage in which they produced a short line of ceramic vases, cigarette sets, candy dishes and wall pockets, all of which were decorated with small handmade roses.

Frank and Wanda Danciart were very pleasant people, very easy to communicate with, and it was clear they were having trouble selling their very limited production. Their representative in a downtown showroom promised large orders but produced very little. There was no foot traffic for retail sales and those who drove by would not stop to look. I knew nothing about ceramics, but believed they were beautiful. With all of the shortages of merchandise during that period, I could not understand why this product would not sell, and when I mentioned that, Frank asked, "Why don't you try it?" I explained my status, but we both agreed neither of us had anything to lose were I to try. I just did not know that salesmen did not work on Saturdays. He advised me of my costs and wholesale prices and my profit margin. My first call was at a hardware store on my way home. There was interest and a first order of $60 for merchandise which cost me $40; a good profit. The next day, Saturday, I sold orders of more than $350 at two stores. Later that day, I obtained another order for just under $400. I had earned profits in the excess of $250.

The decision was relatively easy although it developed, as you would imagine, not quite that simply. I did see the great potential and Sophie was willing to go along with the decision having great faith in me. In 1948, I was doing well enough to make my first real estate investment. I was able to accumulate enough for a down payment on a duplex with two-bedrooms in each unit. We took the lower level and rented the upper level at a figure, even with controlled prices, that was nearly enough to reach my monthly payment. It was perfect timing as Stan was growing up, and we all needed and wanted to have our own place.

Sophie's mother and dad had been great. We did have a beautiful relationship. However, we all realized that they needed peace and quiet, and we needed a home of our own.

We stayed in that house until I took advantage of an offer for veterans and purchased a $10,000 home (2520 Butler) in West Los Angeles just before the birth of Arlene. Selling the duplex made it possible to not only pay off the mortgage of our new home but permitted us to add the lots and Gateway to our holdings. Sophie had a difficult pregnancy with Arlene, but thanks to her sweet mother's care, she could remain in bed for an extended period. I nearly missed Arlene's birth as I was on a business trip in New York. When Sophie started labor, I drove nights and days from New York, nearly getting into an accident driving off the road. I finally got home and Sophie still was in labor.

Occasionally, Sophie and my mother and father would come with me. Fannie and Joe would look after the kids. The first trip Sophie went on, she had to fly alone to New York City. I bought her a ticket three months in advance. Sophie had never flown, and lost weight as she worried about flying in an airplane. Fortunately, on the flight she met a nice man named Uri who put her at ease. We had a wonderful time in New York.

Papel Family. Stanley, Sophie, Phil and Arlene in 1948

Phil and Sophie Papel with business associates. Frank and Wanda Danciart (left) Sam Wilheight with wife (center) circa 1948

I was so involved with my work that I was often traveling away from home, four to six weeks at a time, and missing much of my family life. My children hardly recognized me. Thus, I resigned from my job and decided to open a shop at Walt Disney's new theme park, Disneyland.

> Note: My father, Phil Papel, wrote the story of the first 39 years of his life. Only minor editing was done, and the life story up through that time is told in his own words. From age 39 through his death in 1998 at age 82, his later life story was completed primarily through the memories of his wife, Sophie Papel, and son, Stanley Papel.

I had put most of the energy of my career into the growth and development of Ever Art Ceramics and expanded the facility in my mother's garage into a national company that had broad distribution throughout the United States. My goal was to have some ownership in the company. While I was close with the owner, Frank Danciart, his wife, Wanda, never trusted Jews. It became apparent that I could never have a stake in owning the company. I also had to travel for sales throughout the country, and missed my life with Sophie, Stanley and Arlene. Hence, as time went on, I began looking for another career.

I became an investor in Yona Originals that was founded by Max Lipton and his wife, Yona. Yona was the designer, and Max was the General Manager. My role was to develop sales. It turned out that Max Lipton was a con artist. My investment went all for his own personal use and most of the funds that were invested to grow the company went to Max Lipton's personal gain. I lost a major part of our family savings to the extent that we thought we might have to sell the house. We watched our pennies during this time and I had income from selling other gift lines. However, it was a very (brief) time from when I left Ever-Art Ceramics until the new chapter in my career started that would take me to retirement. This new chapter in my life began thanks to Walt Disney.

Walt Disney had a dream to open a family-friendly theme park promoting his Disney characters. I had already been successful in the wholesale end of the giftware industry, and I believed that a theme park opened by Disney would give me the opportunity to open a retail location directly. When I learned that Walt Disney was developing a major theme park, I was one of the first to express interest in opening a shop at Disneyland, which was set to open in 1955. With Sophie's blessings, I invested our savings into the China and Gift shops to be located on Main Street in Disneyland.

After Disney informed me that he had selected me as a merchant for Disneyland, I was asked to choose a name for the shop. I named his store after actor Charlie Ruggles. In the Paramount Pictures film, If I Had a Million (1932), Ruggles portrayed "Mr. Henry Peabody," a china shop owner who received an unexpected gift of one million dollars from a dying tycoon. In response, Peabody joyfully destroyed all his china and glass in the shop. I paid homage to Ruggles by naming the store Ruggles Gift Shop.

In 1955, I opened two shops on Main Street in Disneyland and was elated that Walt Disney selected me to be in attendance for the opening of the theme park in July. It was a risky proposition for me, as I was required to pay the entire first year lease in advance. Additionally, I had to pay to furnish and decorate my shops in an elegant manner. I hired our manager and salespeople while the entire family helped set up the shop, unpacking the merchandise out of the boxes, meticulously cleaning each item, adding sales tags, and then putting them into carts and onto shelves. Additional glass merchandise was stored at a farm in Garden Grove which was owned by the manager of the store.

I had two shops at Disneyland: China Closet and Ruggles Gift Shop. The China Closet sold primarily fine ceramics and glass. Beautifully colored glass and old-fashioned lamps were featured along with bone china and other more expensive but traditional ceramic home accessories and gifts. Right next door was Ruggles China & Gift Shop that sold popular priced contemporary gift items as well as some souvenirs. I was not allowed to carry souvenirs with the Disney name on them. However, I was permitted to use a label that said Ruggles Disneyland, so I developed items such as The Spinning Fairy (aka Spinning Tinkerbell) which, although not really Tinker Bell, nevertheless resembled the fairy from Peter Pan. She had glowing wings that when blown on would spin around at the register. Eventually these spinning but brittle fairies became scarce and valuable collector's items. I can't imagine how many we sold during the several years of our lease in Disneyland.

One of our best items was a grab bag containing prizes could be purchased for 59 cents or two for a $1. The counter sign read, "Odds much better than Las Vegas." Each bag contained items valued up to $5. Arlene helped wrap the colored grab bags and received a commission of one cent per bag sold. Ruggles Gift Shop also carried $1 raincoats that were popular during on wet days since many tourists did not bring them to usually sunny southern California.

The two shops proved to be a success for me from a financial perspective, and I enjoyed interacting with the customers. I enjoyed working there because I loved children. If a little kid was crying, I would console him or her with a little gift. The signs in the shop read, "Relax, we do not charge for accidental breakage." People appreciated the friendly atmosphere, which made them more likely to purchase an item. Sophie found the family atmosphere pleasant and was delighted to observe customers in the stores. She sat on the open porch in front of shops watching people as they had a grand time in the magical stores on Main Street. Years later a book was published called Little Shop on Main Street by Dave Mason which gave the history of this venture at Disneyland.

For the family, it was fun having Disneyland stores, but it also proved to be difficult on Sophie and the kids who lived in Los Angeles. Prior to the building of a freeway, I drove between Los Angeles and Anaheim more than two hours each way. That limited the time that I had to spend with my family. I kept the family in Los Angeles during the school year because of the proximity to Sophie's family, and I wanted Stan and Arlene to go to school there. Even so, Sophie and I decided to buy a second house in Anaheim, a little G.I. house on Morgan Lane.

During the summers, Sophie and the kids relocated to Anaheim. Sophie enjoyed living there and the entire family pitched in to run my stores during the summer. Arlene made some friends that she played with during the summer months. Stan would spend his days at the store and would take college courses at night at Orange Coast College and Santa Ana College.

Walt Disney liked me and often asked for my advice on business manners. We respected each other, and Disney told his manager to be good to me. But as Disneyland grew and expanded, Walt Disney started taking over ownership of all the retail shops. My stores were one of the last ones to be taken over. Regardless, I felt I was being stabbed in the back.

Arlene and Stan had a strong reaction when they learned that I was being evicted from Disneyland. They wrote a letter to Walt Disney saying how I loved that store and how much it hurt me that I had to relinquish a business that I had put my heart and soul into creating. They mailed the letter and then told Sophie. She reacted in shock saying, "How can you do that? Dad can handle his own business—that's a terrible thing to do." Sophie was so upset that she insisted that Stan try and get the letter back from the mailbox when the postman came to take the mail from it. The kids waited for the postman to come so that they could try to get the letter back, but he said, "Once you put it in the mailbox, it's property of the government and we're not allowed to give it back." Nevertheless, I thought it was very nice of Stan and Arlene to stand up for me and I did not really mind that the kids sent the letter to Disney (photo of actual letter can be seen on the website in the Disney Connection section).

I quickly moved on from Disneyland, developing new success in the retail and wholesale business. In 1962, I established a business where other people bought my items while I would exhibit my products in gift shows all over the country. For example, the crystal toothpick vase, which I bought for twenty cents, would sell wholesale for forty cents, and the retailers would sell it for seventy-nine cents. I sold more than a million crystal toothpick vases. The vases were the major foundation for my miniature crystal line. I also had opened other retail stores. Two stores were located in the Disneyland Hotel and I continued to own them thanks to a lease from the Wrather Corporation. I also established a small chain with Chuck Highland that operated in Ports of Call Village (San Pedro, CA), under the name Hudson Ruggles. We also opened a store in Oceanside and continued to add more stores over the years.

More importantly, though, during the Disneyland years, I further developed my wholesale business, Phil Papel Imports, Inc. I hired salesmen for my company. By the time Stan joined the company in 1970, I had stores in the Disneyland Hotel, Oceanside, Movieland Wax Museum, and Century City. When Stan joined, we opened several gift and souvenir locations together aboard the Queen Mary (docked in Long Beach, CA), and planned to open additional mall shops in Fox Hills (Culver City) and in the Glendale Galleria. In addition to the gift shops, we also purchased and developed the Kitchen Store in Santa Monica Mall and at Pasadena Plaza. These stores pre-dated the larger gourmet kitchen stores that became popular in malls in the later 20th century. In the early 1970's the retail business was earning more than $1,000,000 and the wholesale business grew rapidly at around $750,000 per year.

I continued to travel overseas searching for the latest trends in merchandise, sometimes joined by Sophie. She worked with vendors, wheeling and dealing prices on new products. I also went with Stan on a business trip to England, spending time with my agent in Stoke-on-Trent to import English-made ceramics.

I enjoyed spending time with Sophie. We were a happy couple that respected each other and never argued. I consider myself to be a caring father who loved both of his children, Stan and Arlene. The entire family went on a special family vacation every year.

Family vacations were very important to Sophie and me. While Sophie and I would take vacations for just the two of us, our most important vacations while the kids were growing up included Stan and Arlene. Our most popular destination in the early years with the kids was Las Vegas. While the kids couldn't gamble, they would stand on the sidelines watching everyone

Phil Papel. Owner of Phil Papel Imports circa 1954

dropping their nickels and dimes into the slot machines. They loved the dinner shows, and I would tip the maître d' in order to get good tables. That always impressed the kids! We all enjoyed the shows and the fabulous Flamingo Hotel was our favorite place to stay.

There were lots of other destinations that we also enjoyed. The trip to Yosemite National Park was a favorite. As the kids got older, we took them on longer trips such as Hawaii where we stayed at the Hawaiian Village in Waikiki and at the Coco Palms in Kauai.

After Stan and Arlene married and started their own families, we began taking them, their spouses, and our grandchildren on family cruises. The cruises were family bonding opportunities. It was a wonderful experience for the entire family. I would spend time with each person in the family during the cruise. In Stan's case, I would ask him about his life and give him advice about being a father. I would give pointers for getting along with the kids. Furthermore, I gave him tips on how to balance his business while still spending quality time with the kids. I would ask Stan questions that would make him think. Sophie also spent individual time with her young grandkids, but she remembers them blowing off her advice. I think we took eleven family cruises in all, and that does not even begin to cover the cruises that Sophie and I took alone or with our friends.

Sophie and I had a wonderful group of friends whom we socialized with. One group consisted of four couples who would come over for cocktails. I would rendezvous with my male friends and play gin rummy while Sophie and her female friends played mahjong. Six of us were inseparable in Palm Springs—Jack and Shiffra Levin, Earl and Elaine Himovitz. We bought our first condo in Palm Springs in the late 1960's. Our second condo was purchased in about 1976 and was like a full-size home. The Levins and Himovitzes moved into neighboring units. Arlene and her family, as well as Stan and his family, were frequent visitors. I've encouraged Sophie to keep the place in Palm Springs even after my health started deteriorating.

In Los Angeles we belonged to a group that we called "The Gourmet Club" consisting of nine couples who would get together, meeting at a different home each month. The hostess provided the liquor for cocktails. Then the hostess would designate who would make Hors d'oeuvres while she made the entrée, the main course. Everyone else had to bring a food item, from vegetables to desserts. The women were good cooks and used their own recipes. Each gathering began with a long cocktail hour so that everyone was happy.

The men had a good time drinking while the women cooked. I remember one time someone skinny dipped in the pool. We got pretty wild at some of these parties. Being mostly professionals and all successful people, it would be a time to let our hair down. Several of the couples became very good friends.

We had different themes for each month. When it was Halloween, everyone dressed up in costumes and when it was Valentine's Day, the couples did something with a romantic flair. For Christmas, the Gourmet Club had a holiday theme.

In a sense, the Gourmet Club saved my life. One night in the mid 1950's, I wore a short sleeve shirt, and suddenly noticed a growth on my arm. My friend Dr. Leo Miller asked to see the mole. Leo bluntly told me, "I want you to go to the doctor on Monday." I thought I might have injured my arm at work. Sophie and I were young and naive and did not know how important it was to get it checked out. When I went to UCLA Medical Center, the specialist diagnosed it as melanoma. Fortunately, they discovered it early. I had to have an operation that left a big scar on my forearm, but the melanoma was gone and it never returned. I also had a mole on the bottom of my foot that was benign at the time but could have changed like the one on my arm.

When I was not working or spending precious time with my family, I enjoyed sports. After the Dodgers moved from Brooklyn in 1957 and began playing in Los Angeles in 1958, my best friend Jack Levin and I shared season tickets. I also enjoyed watching baseball on television.

I collected stamps as a young man, dating back to my employment at the post office. I gave Stan my stamp collection, which he still cherishes. I also helped Stan with his coin collection. Each evening I would bring home the change from the shop in Disneyland. Stan would meticulously examine the dates of each coin saving the valuable ones. He would also roll the coins for me which made it easy to deposit them the next day. I know he became an avid coin collector. He found some valuable coins and started buying coins with his savings. I remember Jack said he was nuts to spend $40 on a penny (a 1909-S VDB), but later it was worth over $300. Who knows what it's worth today? (Editor's note: At time of editing in 2019, the 1909-S VDB cent can be valued to $4000 or more depending on condition.)

One of the biggest surprises in Sophie's and my life happened in May 1964 in celebration of our 25th Wedding Anniversary. We were supposed to go out with Steph and Lester Leff and Marian and Eddie Ullman for dinner. But Stephanie made some excuse why we had to return to the house. Low and behold, the house was filled with all of our best friends and relatives. Stan and Arlene answered the door and said: "THIS IS YOUR LIFE!" They put together the most wonderful story along with a beautiful scrapbook. I am hoping some of the pages and the beautiful poem can be incorporated into this book when I finally finish it.

I should put in a few words about my siblings in adult life. There were five of us, all about two years apart. Sol was the oldest, then Bernie, sister Mary, yours truly, and Sid the baby. Sol came off as happy-go-lucky, but he had a mean streak. Bernie was a good boy but he married Ethyl, who argued a lot with everyone, including my mom, Fannie. Sister Mary was always a sweet and fun girl but she married, Al, and I really can't say anything nice about him. I looked after Sid as my only little brother, and we were the closest in the group. There was always some kind of commotion going on in the family but we kept pretty close knit, mostly because Fannie wanted the family to remain close.

Once Stan came into the business, things started to change. My strengths were in being a "people person," having sold products in the industry for so long. Stan's MBA degree enhanced his organizational skills. The majority of the staff could not keep up with him. We had moved from Orange County to South Central Los Angeles when Stan joined the company, but within a few months of Stan starting nearly the entire office staff quit. Stan hired people that he worked with at May Company, and we started to operate like a larger company. The company began to grow. My daughter, Arlene, also came to work with me. She started part-time writing our company newsletter, The Pipeline. Each month she would interview me and write "Phil's Pheelings" which would feature my words of wisdom. It comes with being the "old timer" in the business. Before long, Arlene started running the Custom Design Department of Papel Imports. How proud I was to see my two children working together. A father's dream had come true! It made me very happy to see Stan and Arlene working for the company and carrying it forward into the future.

In the early 1970's we wanted to buy a place in Palm Springs. Figuring that Stan would soon be running the company, it was time to start enjoying our spare time. I said, "We are going to Palm Spring to buy a little house, and I already know which one to buy." There were three model homes, A, B, and C., and I explained to Sophie, "You'll probably like C better, but A is the best one to buy, so let's buy A." We looked at the model and purchased Model A in Canyon Sands. We loved our new Palm Springs home and had fun furnishing it. I also convinced Jack Levin to purchase one of the model homes in the same complex.

While all this was going on with the moves and travel, there was also a lot going on with Arlene's love life and then Stan's love life. Arlene met Jay in about 1970. I know they met at the May Company. They were married in 1971, and Arlene Papel became Arlene Slater. The funny thing was that I was bringing my tuxedo to be altered for Arlene's wedding, and the tailor, Mr. Solomon, said, "Oh, your son is getting married!" I told him it was my daughter. Mr. Solomon then asked, "When is your son getting married?" I said, "When you introduce him to a nice Jewish girl." Bottom line is that he checked in with Joe Miller, who had one unmarried daughter. Even though there was a ten-year age difference, they met and quickly fell in love.

Arlene was married in 1971. The next year Stan was married. Then the grandchildren started coming! First Stan and Aileen gave birth to a beautiful baby daughter, Melissa. The following year, Arlene gave birth to our first grandson, Bradley. In 1976, Stan and Aileen proudly welcomed a son, Evan. Arlene and Jay welcomed a daughter in 1978. Then a long span, but a wonderful addition to our family was the birth of Stan's second daughter Dara in 1986, completing the dream of having not only a beautiful wife, and two lovely children, but also five wonderful grandchildren.

I enjoyed working less hours and spending more time with my beloved Sophie. We really enjoyed going to Palm Springs However, we quickly outgrew the unit at Canyon Sands, and a few years later we bought a much larger place which was to be our where we spent the rest of our years in Palm Springs.

About the same time as we bought the condo in Palm Springs, we gifted the house on Cashmere Terrace to Arlene and her husband Jay. Concurrently we bought a condo in West Los Angeles on Greenfield. It was adequate for us as we were ready to downsize. It had a very nice-sized living room and dining room. The master bedroom was on one side of the unit and the guest bedroom, which I used as my office, was on the other side. We are basically spending Monday through Thursday in Los Angeles, and Thursday through Sunday in Palm Springs. It's a good life, and I can't complain. Plus, Sophie and I are doing a lot of travel together. It's a busy semi-retired life.

When Melissa was three months old, Stan and Aileen went on a trip. Adele said they would watch Melissa for a week and Sophie and I would watch them for a week. After Adele's week was up, she came over with all the bottles and swings but she did not tell Sophie what a big job it was to take care of Melissa. Sophie had to call a pediatrician to find out why Melissa was vomiting and subsequently modified her baby formula.

Phil and Sophie Papel at JHA (Jewish Home for Aged) circa 1997

STANLEY PAPEL CONTINUES WITH HIS FATHER'S STORY: ON NOVEMBER 2, 1998, PHIL PAPEL Passed away from complications related to Alzheimer's. The last several years of my father's life were difficult, with the changes due to Alzheimer's. However, Phil will always be remembered for the vibrant years and the love and happiness he brought to others.

His daughter, Arlene, wrote the following:

I've been asked to say a little about what kind of dad Phil was to me. I'm not one to write a lot about something that is really very private. I will say this. I feel I had the most wonderful and perfect father in the entire universe. He had a wonderful sense of humor, but he was sensitive and wise and loved by all.

Before I turned 5 years old, I remember during a walk, he told me I had to go to college just in case I may have to help support my family one day. When I was 6, he went to my first-grade teacher to tell her I was having nightmares trying to make a wooden tugboat. He said since I wasn't going to grow up and build boats, I shouldn't have to finish the boat (we used saws and hammers and nails in those days at age 6). He returned back home to tell me he didn't get his way because the real lesson was not about the boat...it was to finish what I had started. The ugliest tugboat remained in our back porch for years as a symbol of that lesson as well as how hard he tried to help me.

When I was 11 and graduated elementary school, he wrote in my autograph book to always stand up for my rights when I knew I was right, but never be afraid to say I was sorry if there was a chance that I was wrong. When I went to Berkeley at a time when many parents would not allow their children to go there due to political demonstrations, he told me that he and my mom were proud to send me there. He said if he ever got a phone call one day that I had been taken to jail while demonstrating, as long as it was something I believed in, I would have his support! When I graduated college, he told me I could be and do anything I wanted in the world. When I had personal conflicts, he told me that most problems were self-inflicted and self-answerable...and he was right!

When I became a mother, he became a grandfather to my children and he was cherished and loved so very much. It is beautiful to see the forever loving memories he has given three entire generations.

When my dad had Alzheimer's Disease for the last 10 years of his life, I learned new lessons about love during my weekly visits. One day towards the end of his struggle, I was alone in the hospital room with him and I just put my head on his chest and cried and cried. Even in his last days, he managed to lift his arm and try to comfort me by rubbing my back. My dad was my friend, my hero and my mentor. I think of him every single day and feel so thankful that some- how he was my dad.

Today, I still work full-time as a Vice President of Product Development for a very large giftware company. I am happily married, have two wonderful children and four beautiful grandchildren. I feel my dad's guidance and love all the time.

The following tributes were offered at Phil's funeral service:

A Letter to Phil Papel

Written by his friend, Jack A. Levin

NOVEMBER 11, 1994

When we were together recently, we had a really good belly laugh remembering how we stacked the deck on Buddy. We had arranged the cards so that you were dealt a pat gin hand and Buddy got the highest possible count. I'll never know how you and I kept a straight face while he, in consternation, counted the almost 100 points, plus gin, that he saw in his hand.

It was such a fond memory, one of so many we have experienced together in the 50 years we've been friends. It started me thinking many more.

Remember in 1946 when each of us was looking for vacant lots on which to build our first home? You counseled me (no, you ordered me) not to buy one that I had seen and liked because it already had some concrete foundation on it which would have cost a lot of money to remove. Of course, it was on a G.I. Loan and my monthly payment was $53.68. Yours must have been almost the same.

In 1950 when you were in Chicago on a business trip, I called you in the middle of the night and asked you to buy a good used late model Cadillac for me, and drive it home. And you actually did it, through rain and sleet and snow.

How from time to time you would take me with you to visit your mother. She was a very special lady.

How about when Arlene was born. You and Sophie named me as her godfather.

How you taught me how to play gin. And you are still taking my money.

How when you bought a home in Palm Springs and wouldn't leave me alone until we bought one too. And then when you sold the first and bought a new one at Canyon one at Canyon Sands, you wouldn't hear of anything but that I would buy one there as well. (It was one of the best buys of my life). And then you called Earl and told him you had put a deposit on one for him and he ended up buying one also.

How at a party at my home in Cheviot Hills, Leo Miller saw a growth on your arm (it turned out to be a melanoma) and together shared the experience of your surgery and sweating out the years afterwards praying it wouldn't return. And it didn't.

How in 1947, we (with Sophie and Shiffra) were on our way to the Highland Springs Resort. I was driving and we had just decided we were on a leisurely, relaxing vacation when I got a ticket for speeding. And even though you said you wouldn't do it, you shared paying the fine.

How in 1945, you and Earl and I joined the B'nai B'rith together. And we've been The Musketeers ever since.

How from time to time over the last 50 years, we would have a disagreement about something or other, and after talking it out we would end up loving each other more than ever.

How I taught you everything you know about good barbecuing.

How every time we would pass a telephone, we would reach in the coin return to see if any coins were there. Shades of the Depression.

How after I got my Boxer dog Dandy, and you saw how sweet and gentle she was, you got a Boxer for Stan and Arlene and called her Taffy.

How after Shiffra and I gave you and Sophie a 25th anniversary party, you reciprocated by treating us to a trip and to confuse us, you drove in circles for 30 minutes before we finally arrived at the airport and boarded a flight to San Francisco.

How when Shiffra and I were remarried on our 25th anniversary, you were my best man.

How after Shiffra's death, when Juanita and I married, you were my best man once again.

How when I became a Bar Mitzvah in 1977, you gave a loving speech of congratulations.

How we, our wives, and the Himovitzes have been together almost every New Year's Eve in the last 50 years.

How each of us teasingly insults the other, which insults are really expression of the love and respect we have for each other.

How at a gift show 15 or 20 years ago, you saw an expensive antique music box you wanted to buy, but didn't have the ready cash. You borrowed it from me and now that I think about it, I'm not sure you paid me back.

How we've shared good times and bad, never being judgmental or exerting undue pressure on the other…to.be… or to do… or to say something either not in our character or something neither of us was unwilling or unable (for whatever reason) to do.

I could go on and on remembering, so the next time we get together, we can reminisce some more.

Phil, I just wanted you to know that our friendship has given the word a very special meaning and that you've been a very important part of my life. Thanks for always being there.

Please give your dear Sophie a hug and a kiss for me.

Love, Jack

Eulogy for Philip Papel

by his son, Stan Papel

*"Some people come into our lives and quickly go
Some stay for a while, leave footprints on our hearts,
And, we are never ever the same."*

This was written by Flavia, a friend and colleague of my Dad's and licensed on giftware items of my dad's company. I think when she wrote it, she must have had my dad in mind because he is one of those people who leave footprints on our hearts forever. He is loved by so many relatives, friends, and people who he has known through business. He has made a difference in so many peoples' lives and will continue to live on in our hearts and memory.

While the last several years have not been typical of my dad's life, they have given our family the time to adjust, reflect, and appreciate the attributes of a most loving husband to my mother, father to Arlene and me, and grandfather to Melissa, Brad, Evan, Kim and Dara.

Last week I went into my office to look for a book for an assignment I had. Among the books was this untitled book that aroused my curiosity. Opening the book, I remembered it was the story of my dad's life, which he wrote in 1982. I'd like to read a short portion related to my dad meeting my mom.

"My social life was becoming more interesting as I naturally did some dating but really had no special person that held my attraction. On a Saturday night, June 27, 1936, a very close friend called to ask my plans for the evening. It was at that party that I met Sophie Roth and was immediately attracted to her. The only problem was that my friend appeared to be interested in her as well.

I don't believe it necessary to reveal details of our long courtship. That date, other than my birth, has to be recorded as the most important day of my life. Nothing of what lies ahead could have been accomplished if her love, confidence, and trust had not been there. Sophie was involved in all the decision-making of every significant move in addition to being an inspiration. She has always been there to involve herself with good advice and the sincere deep desire to help in any fashion. Had there been a dedication of this story of my life, certainly it would be to Sophie."

My sister and I have been so fortunate to be raised in a family with so much love. My father truly loved my mom with all of his heart, and that love was enough to share with his children, grandchildren, relatives, and friends. Dad truly loved people and I know so many people loved him. Whether it was a business venture, playing gin rummy with his friends, cruises with his family, charitable activities, he enjoyed and appreciated people who were part of his life. He touched many lives and has made footprints in so many peoples' hearts.

For me, I remember after WWII he showed me the ceramic factory in my Bubbe's garage that started his career in the giftware industry. I remember as a child running out of the doctor's office when it was my turn to get a shot. My mom couldn't catch me, and later my dad brought me back to the doctor to apologize. We remember all the family trips made and the films my dad took and later put on video cassettes so that Arlene and I could have copies. We remember all the family get-togethers. I remember his first shop in Disneyland where my sister and I would wrap grab bags.

I remember Phil Papel Imports, which was an important part of his life as well as a career for many people including me. I remember back in 1984 how I got the company into pretty deep trouble, and it was my father who was there to help me out… and, he told me he would always be there for me if I needed him. I remember how much he loved his mother and how he took such good care of her in her later years. I remember the many cruises with his children and grandchildren and how Dad would spend special time with each of us. I remember when he first had Alzheimer's and I wanted to tell him how much I loved him… and he held my hand said, "I know." But most of all, we remember a totally beautiful person who gave of himself to others with such love in his heart. I only hope I can pass that love to people in my life.

I'd like to share something else. When I was growing up, my father used to give me lots of advice. At times, I didn't always like the advice he gave me. And, then when I was twenty-something, I began to realize that there was a lot of wisdom in what he said and I began to seek his advice. During the past few years, there have been many times when I needed to turn to my dad for his words of wisdom. I found by asking him, verbally or in mind, I could receive those good answers as though he was talking to me. It helped me through a difficult time and I know he will help me through the rest of my life. Perhaps this is what is called spirit, because he will be with me whenever I need him. I know right now he is saying to me… "This is not a time to grieve. It is a time to celebrate my life. I have had a good life and done everything I've wanted to do in my lifetime. I have loved and been loved…then…he is reminding me to make sure that Mom is always okay. And Dad is telling me to tell Dara that he will be with us when she lights the candle for him at her Bat Mitzvah next year.

I will miss you Dad, but I know that you are still with us.

IN LOVING REMEMBRANCE
*Beloved Husband
Father and Grandfather*

PHILIP S. PAPEL
August 17, 1916–November 2, 1998

ALWAYS IN OUR HEARTS
*As Long As We Live,
He Too Shall Live*

PART III
Sophie Roth Papel
(1918–)

ANCESTRY CHART FOR SOPHIE ROTH

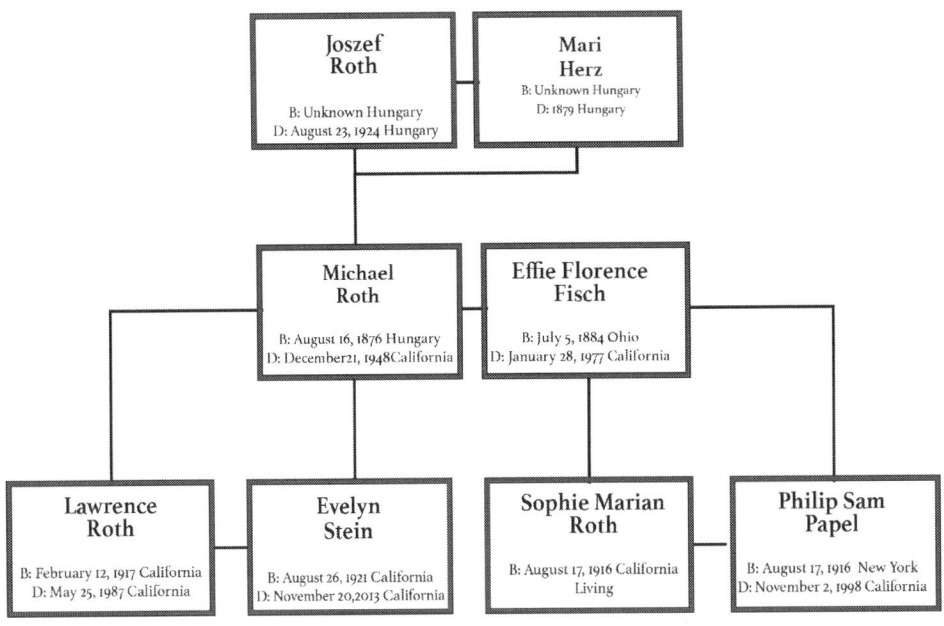

INTRODUCTION

Sophie Roth Papel
(1918–)

Introduction by Stanley Papel

December 2019

As I add this introduction to the life story of my mom, Sophie Papel, she is a happy 101-year-old and still going strong.

Sophie Papel wrote an autobiography for an English class in 1933 as a 15-year-old student. She titled the autobiography "Fifteen Years on Parade."

For the years after age 15, there are three major eras:

- The time until Sophie Roth married Phil Papel in 1939.
- The years that Sophie and Phil were married from 1939 until 1998 when Phil Papel passed away.
- From 1998 until Present (December 2019)

Fifteen Years on Parade

by Sophie Papel

Foreword

In this book, I live over my experiences from my babyhood through my fifteenth year. When first entering upon the task of this work, I did not feel that is would be very exciting, but I find that it has been of great interest to me, and I hope will also be to my readers.

CHAPTER 1

SOPHIE ROTH PAPEL
BIRTH AND BABYHOOD (B. 1918)

Two days before Armistice Day, on November 19, 1918, I was born at Angeles Hospital in Los Angeles, California. I was named Sophie Marian Roth, Sophie after my maternal grandmother, and Marian after my father's mother.

My father, Mike Roth, was born in Hungary. He came to the United States when he was 20 years old, became a citizen as soon as he possibly could, and has been a loyal American ever since. My mother, Effie, was born in Cincinnati, Ohio. Her maiden name was Fisch and she came from a very prominent family.

My parents told me that I caused them very little trouble as a baby, and that after I was one month old, I slept the whole night through without waking up at all. I am the youngest in the family and have only one brother. He is only 21 months older than I am and we have always been the greatest of playmates.

My father and I were always pals. He tells me that one of his greatest pleasures was rocking and singing me to sleep when I was a baby. When I got a little older, I could hardly wait until he got home from his work. My brother and I would wait outside for him and would run up to meet him. After our dinner, he would play hide and seek and other games with us. My mother always had us take a long nap in the afternoon, so that we could stay up until about eight o'clock in the evening.

My mother and I also were great pals. I would go to her with all my childhood troubles and she would comfort me. Of course, my mother was busy with her household duties and did not have as much time to play with us as my father did.

When I was a baby, my father bought two dozen hens. He said the money we saved from the eggs they laid should be put in a bank account for me. I felt that the chickens were my personal property and made pets of them.

Before I was old enough to go to school, I had a great many toys and would pass my time playing with them. Of all my toys, I liked my dolls the best. I had a large collection of dolls and liked to make clothes for them.

When I was little, I always wanted to own a puppy or kitten. My mother had the idea that animals carry diseases, so I had to content myself with stuffed animals. This, as far as I remember, was the greatest disappointment of my early days.

Sophie and Larry Roth circa 1921

CHAPTER 2

SOPHIE ROTH PAPEL
BEGINNING SCHOOL (1918–)

When I was almost five years old, my mother took me to kindergarten at the Arlington Heights Elementary school. She stayed with me the first day and I enjoyed it very much. The second day, she took me again and was going to leave me there. I started to cry when she was about to leave and said I would stay there without her. My mother did not believe in forcing me to stay. She told me she was busy and had to go home. She said I did not have to stay if I did not want to, but I could come home with her. At home, she gave me a good talk. She said that when children are old enough to go to school, they go and stay without their mothers and told me to let her know when I thought I was old enough to go. She told me she would take me there and call for me. My father, on the other hand, tried to bribe me into going. He promised to buy me a big box of candy as soon as I would go. I stayed at home for one month and then told my mother I thought I was old enough to go to and stay there alone. I also reminded my father about his promise and enjoyed my box of candy. I enjoyed kindergarten very much and loved my teacher. On the last day of school, my teacher said she did not know what she would do without me. This made me very proud indeed.

It was in the first grade that my troubles really began. As a small child, I was very timid and bashful. I had the habit of crying and if I did not understand something, or if the teacher would scold me in front of the class, I would start to cry. My first-grade teacher was determined to break me of this bad habit. Once she sent me out of the room into the hall. Another time she sent me to the principal. This greatly frightened me. My teacher won. I was afraid to cry because I did not want to be sent to the principal again. However, it was very hard for me to keep from crying.

The biggest tragedy of my early childhood occurred when I was four years old. My brother was six years old. Neither one of us had even been away from home without my mother. My brother had been very sick with ear abscesses for about a month. One morning when I woke up, instead of seeing my mother, I saw my aunt. She told me that my brother had developed a mastoid and that the doctor had taken him early that morning to the hospital for an operation. After breakfast, she took me to her house to stay for the next 10 days. My mother stayed with my brother at the hospital day and night. I missed my mother and brother very much.

Three days after his operation, my aunt took me to the hospital to see my brother. He and I were both so affected; we could not speak to each other at first. After a little while, we both started to laugh and soon became our natural selves again. My brother recovered very rapidly, and we were soon back at home again.

CHAPTER 3

SOPHIE ROTH PAPEL
TERRORS (1918–)

When I was three years old, we were living at the beach. I was standing on the front lawn, when all at once I saw a dog running towards me. I did not think anything of it. I just stood there watching that dog, when all of the sudden, he got to our apartment house and gave one jump on me. I started to scream thinking that I was half-killed. My mother came running out when she heard my cries and when I told her about the dog running and jumping on me and licking my face, she explained to me that is the way a dog plays. Well, that is my first terrifying remembrance in life. I suppose the reason I remember it is because it gave me such a scare.

When I was four years old, I really had the scare of my life. We were down at Ocean Park eating in a restaurant. My mother gave me a nickel and told me to go out in front of the restaurant and buy an ice cream cone and that she would wait for me inside. I started out but went on the pier to buy my ice cream. I walked on and on, and the first thing I knew I was lost. I was very worried and kept on looking for my mother, but as I could not find her, I began to cry. A very kind woman came over and helped me look for my mother. She gave me some candy and tried to comfort me. As there was nothing else she could do for me, she called a policeman and turned me over to him.

The policeman was very kind to me, but that did not help matters any for me, and I cried harder than ever. The policeman was about to take me the police station on the back of his motorcycle. This greatly terrified me. However, he decided to call up the station first to see if anyone had inquired for me. To my great relief, he told me that my parents were waiting in front of a certain dry goods store on Ocean Front. He walked with me over to where they were. Oh, how happy I was to see my mother and father again. I was never so scared in all my life, and for a long time after that, when down at the beach, I hung on to my mother's hand.

At the time of the Long Beach earthquake, I happened to be walking on the street with my chum. We stopped and looked in the window of a printing shop on Third Avenue (Los Angeles). All of a sudden, the window started shaking, and we thought this was caused by the machinery. The sidewalk then seemed to move back and forth. People yelled for us to get away from the window and to come into the street. In the morning, I was greatly shocked to learn how many lives had been lost and how much damage had been done. My father has two stores on the main street in Watts. The morning after the earthquake, he received a telephone message to come there as the building was damaged. When he came home, he told us that buildings all around his property were demolished, but that he was very lucky as his damages would not come to very much.

CHAPTER 4

SOPHIE ROTH PAPEL
JOYOUS MEMORIES (1918–)

I am sure every small child is greatly excited around Christmas time, especially when he believes in Santa Claus. I will never forget how thrilled I was to get up early in the morning and find my stocking, which I had hung up empty the night before near the fireplace, all full of good things, the floor all filled with neatly wrapped presents, and the great Christmas tree fully decorated from top to bottom. It was great fun to open my presents, one by one, joyous and happy over each and everyone one of them. My brother received just has many presents as I did. First, he would open one of his, and then I would open one of mine. We would keep this up until we finished opening all our presents. I would call in my many little friends to show them my presents. I remember, I would try to keep awake in bed to get a peek at Santa Claus, and in the morning was very angry with myself for having fallen asleep before he got here.

Halloween is another time that I greatly enjoyed in my younger days. At night my brother and I would walk down Pico Street soaping windows, all dressed up in some silly costumes but which we thought were pretty swell when we were little. My mother and father, of course, would be right behind us all the time. We carried pumpkins with the faces cut out and candles burning inside. We would shove these at people and think that we frightened them very much. One Halloween, my mother put on one of my father's suits when she walked with us. We passed my aunt, uncle, and cousins on the street. They did not recognize her and this greatly amused all of us. The last few Halloweens, we did not fool around and have fun in this way, but instead were invited to parties and had fun playing different games.

Each year I always looked forward to the Fourth of July. Our family would all get together either at our house or at one of my aunt's. We would all bring our fireworks and shoot them off at night. One Fourth of July, we were living at Hermosa Beach. All of a sudden, in the middle of the afternoon, we heard one bang after another. Someone had accidentally thrown a firecracker at a firecracker stand and all the fireworks went off at once. This was very exciting indeed.

Easter, Thanksgiving, Christmas night, and New Year's Eve are always very enjoyable occasions for me. We usually get together at some relative's house and have a big family dinner.

When I was 13 years old, some girls and I formed a club. We used to meet each Friday evening at the home of a Mrs. Martin, a Sunday School teacher of one of my friends. Each girl would bring some kind of food and we would cook it and eat our dinner there. Last summer, Mrs. Martin went to the World's Fair at Chicago, so we did not continue the club. Later we

Sophie Roth. Elementary School Years circa 1926

formed a club, which consisted of both boys and girls. We meet once a week and at least once a month, go on beach parties, theater parties, or house parties. We have special topics for each meeting and at each meeting, a different member takes charge. I enjoy this club very much and I am sure the other members enjoy it as much as I do.

Most of the members of this club also meet each Thursday evening for basketball. We play different teams at times. At other times, the boys play against the girls. It is very good exercise and we all have a very good time.

CHAPTER 5

SOPHIE ROTH PAPEL
VACATIONS (1918–)

There is nothing as comforting and restful, as to be on a vacation, where it is cool in the hot summertime. When my brother and I were small, we used to spend our vacations at the beach, where could play in the sun, and have the healthful ocean breeze to keep us cool all the time. There was nothing I liked better than to play in the water and the wet sand. I sat in the wet sand by the hour digging deep holes, making tunnels, sandcastles and other things one can make in the sand. Vacations at the beach were always a lot of fun for me and to this day, I like nothing better than to go down to the beach, take a long swim and then dry in the scorching sun.

When I was six years old, my mother, my aunt, my little four-year-old cousin, my 14-year old, my brother and I went up to Seven Oaks, intending to stay there for two or three weeks. We went to San Bernardino on a Pacific Electric car and then the rest of the way on the bus. The bus was the most exciting part of the trip for me. I would wind around mountain roads, going up and up, at the rate of about 15 miles per hour. It was such a narrow road, that I knew another car could not pass us if it came along. Looking down below us was the most beautiful view I had ever seen. There were trees all over all the different shades of green that looked so smooth and peaceful swaying with the soft breeze I thought if the bus should fall over the cliff, it would not hurt us very much. Well, the bus did not fall off the cliff. When we arrived at Seven Oaks, my big cousin was sick to her stomach and it made her much sicker to see my little cousin and I go on the swings as soon as we got there.

We had two small log cabins, which, at first, I thought were very nice. My mother, my big cousin, and my brother had one cabin, and my aunt, my little cousin and I had the other. In the evening, we heard a loud bell ringing. I could not imagine what it was, but soon found that it was the dinner bell. I had such an appetite that I ate everything put before me. In the cabins, we had to use oil lamps, which I thought were much more wonderful than electric lights.

When I was ready for bed, I saw what seemed to be millions of spiders, mostly daddy long legs, all over the walls and roof of the cabin and even on the bed. My cousin and I are deathly afraid of spiders. We would not go to bed until we thought they were all killed. I felt sorry for my mother because I know she does not like spiders either.

I usually do not sleep well the first night in a strange bed, but I never slept sounder than I did that night. I woke up early in the morning, and to my horror saw just as many spiders as I saw the night before. I had a very queer feeling that spiders were crawling all over me in the night in order to get up to the roof.

We had a fair breakfast, but not as good as I expected. Later that morning, the proprietor told us to go over to the cow stables, where the men were going to milk the cows. She gave each child a glass to get some fresh milk. I had never seen a cow being milked before, and so I was all eyes. We were anxiously and patiently waiting for our milk, when all of a sudden, the cow's tail went into the bucket of milk, and there were hundreds of flies flying around the poor cow. The man poured out a glass of milk for each of us. It did not seem at all appetizing to me. The milk was warm and thick and had the most sickening taste. It was terrible. I was very disappointed and, after one taste, threw the rest away. After this, my mother had a hard time getting me to drink milk.

We stayed two days at Seven Oaks and then got so tired of it that we decided to go on up to Big Bear Lake.

What a difference between the two places! We stopped at the "Tavern." There was one main hotel building and a few separate bungalows. My mother and aunt decided to stay in a bungalow. It was so neat and clean and had three separate bedrooms in it. We had the most delicious meals in the Tavern dining room. The proprietors, Mr. and Mrs. Brush, were lovely people, and all the guests seemed just like one big family. Mrs. Brush seemed to love all of us children and could not do enough for us. In the evenings, we would have marshmallow toast in front of a big log fire. We went on picnics and many interesting bus rides, and each time Mrs. Brush would have a lovely big lunch packed for us.

While at Big Bear, we visited the Silver Fox farm, the Lucky Baldwin Gold Mine, and many other interesting places. I enjoyed all of these trips and will never forget them. I wish I had time to tell about each of them in detail. We also took a boat trip around the lake, which I liked very much.

When our time was up, I was very sorry to leave Big Bear Lake. However, I was also anxious to get home to see my father and to tell him about all the wonderful trips we had taken.

Three years ago, I spent my vacation at Catalina Island. This was my first visit there. I found it an ideal place to swim and rest. While at Catalina, I went on the glass bottom boat, took the flying fish trip, the Seal Rock trip, and a boat trip to the Isthmus. We also visited the bird farm, the St. Catherine Hotel, the Casino, and the Wrigley home. I greatly enjoyed all of these trips.

I am looking forward to another vacation at Catalina this summer.

Sophie Roth. Confirmation from B'nai B'rith (Jewish Synagogue) in 1933

CHAPTER 6

SOPHIE ROTH PAPEL
BEYOND THE SCHOOL YEARS (1918–)

Interview with Sophie Papel from October 4, 2015; transcribed by Stan Papel

My Chicago-born mother always took good care of me. She was a wonderful cook and she sometimes sacrificed herself so that I could have nice things such as patent leather shoes. My father, who was born in Hungary, was very sweet and also a good cook. He liked to prepare Hungarian-style food and knishes. He was also a strong guy. When I was small, he would hold out his arm and I would swing on it, back and forth.

When I was thirteen, I used to walk from my home on Third Avenue to school at Mount Vernon Junior High School, which I liked. I had a wonderful teacher there, Mrs. McKinnon, whom I'll never forget. I'll always remember her motto in life: "Find a way and make it." I've used that expression all my life; it's helped me so much. If I ever had a problem, I'd find a way and I'd solve it. So, Mrs. McKinnon had a big influence on my life with this expression, which I've shared with others. My daughter Arlene even had her boss make a sign and post it with this life motto.

Then I went to L.A. High School where I had good memories with friends, especially my next-door neighbor Lucille. We both belonged to the Young People's Hebrew Association (YPHA). Once I noticed a small mole on her leg, but she didn't pay any attention to it. It turned out to be cancerous, and she died when we were in high school. It was terrible for me.

Just after I graduated high school in May of 1936, I met my future husband, Phil. It happened this way: I was invited to a party at a girlfriend's house, which at first, I didn't want to attend. Well, I changed my mind and my brother drove me over there. Phil and his friend Nate didn't have any plans that night, so Phil told him, "Let's go to this party at this girl's house. She told me to come." And Nate said okay. The hostess then called them and asked them to bring another girl, and my brother dropped me off at the party house. He was to pick me up when I was ready to leave. But after Phil and I met, Phil agreed to drive me home. Phil had an old car, which he named "Sophie" after we started to date. On the ride back to my house Nate sat in the back seat with me and the girl they had picked up and brought to the party sat in the front with Phil.

The next week, my doorbell rang, and it was Phil. He said, "I'd like to take you out." He couldn't call ahead because he didn't have my phone number, but he remembered the hydrangeas growing on my house's front porch. We went out that night and danced at one of the dance halls near the beach at Ocean Park in Santa Monica. We enjoyed each other a lot and we started to date. Even so, I didn't stop dating other men although he thought I had. He hadn't yet asked me to go steady, so I was still seeing other men. (Like mother, like son!) We usually went out on Saturdays, but one time he asked me out on a different night. At that time, I told him I was seeing other men, and that upset him greatly.

I was still living at home and attending a junior college. During the summer when I wasn't in school, I worked part-time at Bullocks in the gift-wrapping department.

Phil and I dated for three years. You see, he had just bought a new car and he wanted to pay it off, so the marriage question didn't come up. But I told him that we should get married because all my friends were. I proposed to him, and we made a date for a wedding in 1939.

One funny thing happened at the wedding ceremony which was held at the hall of my father's club. One of my cousins who liked to pull jokes put fake dog poop on the white entry carpet. My Aunt Hattie ran and picked it up before we walked down the aisle. Also, my father gave me a good piece of advice. "Sophie, if you ever have a fight with Phil, don't come to me or your mother. Work it out with Phil. And never go to bed mad at each other." I'm a lover, not a fighter by nature, so this was good advice.

After we married, we lived in small apartment close to Silver Lake. But after a burglar tried to break into it, we decided to move. We found a cute little garage apartment on Silver Lake Boulevard. During our early married years, Phil was a mailman; a "happy" one, always whistling. People liked him a lot. When World War II started, he was very lucky. Being a mailman, he was sent by the Navy to be in charge of a post office on a small island near Catalina. I was living again with my mother and father then, and Stanley was a baby only six months old, but Phil got weekend leaves to be with us.

It was at this time that he got the idea to retrieve sailors' duffle bags, which they had thrown away after basic training, repair them by hand, and re-sell them. One day while on leave, he passed an Army-Navy surplus store and convinced them to buy the refurbished duffle bags which he brought to them in his truck. As a result, he got into the duffle bag business, and he made quite a bit of money on the side.

After the war, Phil remained with the postal service but with a better, higher-paying job sorting mail on a railway car. He had to leave the house each morning by 3 AM, and I would get up with him, make him breakfast, and go back to bed. During the day I took care of young Stanley. Now, there was a garage at the house which my family had rented to someone who was storing ceramic gifts in it. Phil saw these items and felt he could also make a living selling ceramics, which fairly quickly became a big company. Phil was a good salesman; he was honest; he didn't overload his customers with too much merchandise. He was always an entrepreneur full of ideas. He made that little business into a factory occupying four blocks: Ever-Art Ceramics.

Elaine and Earl, and Jack and Shiffra became good friends who became an important part of my life. I met both Elaine and Shiffra before they were married, Elaine in junior college, and Shiffra through a mutual friend. At the time I met Elaine she was living with her aunt in the Wilshire district near the museum. I knew Shiffra before she married and remember when she met Jack at the Ambassador Hotel.

As for raising my children, I remember Stan was awfully cute, but liked to get his own way. I used to secretly watch Stan in his crib; he wouldn't go to sleep but would stand up and bounce around. Once Stan didn't want to go to bed and started to cry. My brother was over at the time, and he told me not to go to Stan but just let him cry. If I go to him, I'll spoil him. Sure enough, Stan stopped crying and went to sleep. Arlene was also cute. She would wake up with a smile and was always happy as a child. Stan and Arlene mostly got along, but Stan didn't want his sister to bother him so much, especially when he got older.

We had a house on Cashmere Terrace. Phil bought the lot without telling me about it. He just knew it was a good neighborhood. Anyway, we built the house and hired a contractor whose name was William Tell. During the construction Phil was traveling, so I had a lot to do, going over there and checking to see that everything was being done right. It turned out to be a good home and we lived there for forty years. Because Phil liked to barbecue, we had a barbecue grill right in the kitchen, which shared its chimney with the fireplace. Then, once the kids were grown, we realized that we didn't need such a big house. So, in the early 1970's Phil and I moved from Cashmere Terrace to a west-side condo, and we gave the house to Arlene while giving the family business to Stan. Since then Arlene has remodeled the house. It's very modern now.

While the business grew, I had to frequently go out of town with Phil and my mother came over to take care of the children. Some of these trips were by car. Although I didn't work after I married, I occasionally would keep the books for the family business until it grew too big for me. We occasionally took family trips to Las Vegas and Palm Springs. When I was young, I especially enjoyed going to Ocean Park with my mother and staying at the Cadillac Hotel, where we had an oceanfront room. We had cousins, the Feldsteins, who also rented a room down the block, and we got to see them. My father didn't like to travel but stayed home and cooked for himself.

After I was married, Palm Springs, which Phil loved, became an important part of our life and we bought a condo there at Canyon Sands. After Phil retired, we would go there on Monday and come back to LA on Thursday, to spend the weekend there. Later we bought a larger, nicer place, across from Smoke Tree. We even put a deposit down for our close friends, Elaine and Earl Himovitz, on a condo in the same complex where we owned. Being very surprised, they said, "If you want us there that much, we might as well go along with it." Jack and Shiffra Levin, also bought into the same Condo development. The boys would play gin rummy and Shiffra, Elaine and I would play mahjong with a group of women in our condo complex.

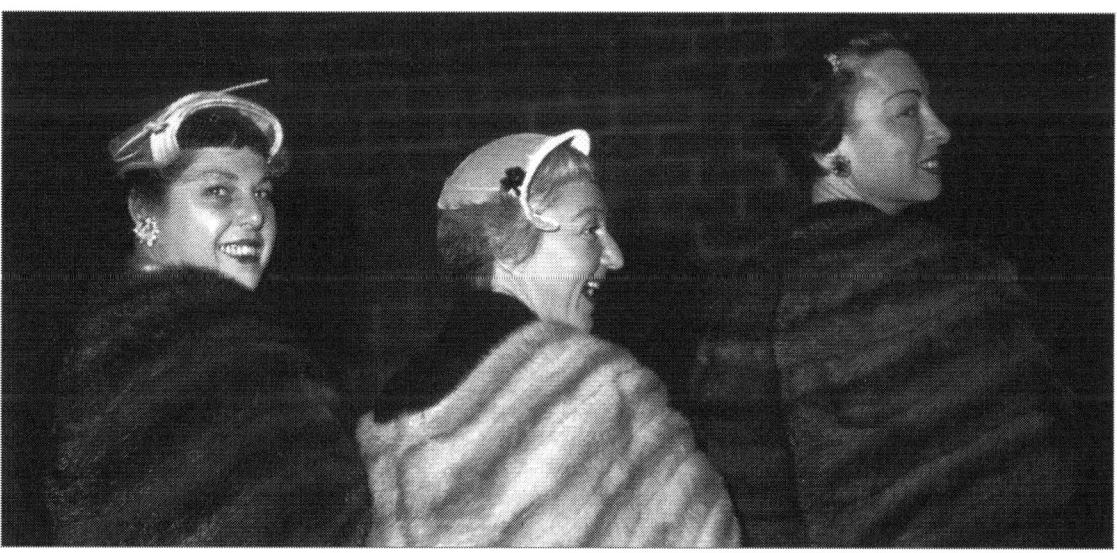

Sophie Roth (right) with best friends, Elaine Himovitz (left) and Shiffra Levin (center) in 1955

We also enjoyed going to San Francisco and staying at San Francisco Suites, where we owned a time-share. We drove up there, stopping along the way in San Luis Obispo and Carmel, and stayed for part of a week. Of course, there were the cruises we went on, with Phil and sometimes with the whole family including Arlene's and Stan's families.

Sophie Papel (center) with cousins, Marian Ullman (left, daughter of Fannie Cohen) and Stephanie Leff (right, daughter of Hattie Blume) circa 1983

The last years of Phil's life were very difficult when he was diagnosed with Alzheimer's disease. He just wasn't himself, and there wasn't anything anyone could do about it. I enrolled in a class to help me understand what was going on with Phil. I learned that whatever Phil did he couldn't help it since he wasn't "Phil" anymore. This class really helped me. Even before the diagnosis, I suspected something wasn't right. He would lose things. Once he returned to a parking lot after a trade show, couldn't find his car, and insisted that it had been stolen.

Phil and I had been married for just under 60 years when he passed away in November 1998; just days before my 80th birthday. It was a dilemma at first whether or not I should have the birthday celebration that Stan and Arlene had planned for me at the Four Seasons in Beverly Hills. However, I knew that Phil would have wanted me to not cancel the party and it was such a good occasion to have my entire immediate family, close relations and best friends together at a time when we all needed to be together.

Sophie Papel. 90th Birthday on November 9, 2008

As this story of my life is being concluded for the book, I am a happy 101-year-old. Arlene has remarried to a wonderful man, Jim Waldrop. Stan has been married for one year now to Sven Wulf, who has become like another son to me. Dara just announced that in 2020 she will be married to Todd Weinger. He is a wonderful addition to our family. I have 8 beautiful great grandchildren, 5 grandchildren who I am proud of, each and every one of them. I am lucky to have the closeness with both Stan and Arlene. I live in the same condo that Phil and I bought together in the early 70's, and I have two wonderful caretakers who are also my close friends. Most importantly, I have had a wonderful marriage for 59 years. It's been a beautiful life.

Sophie Papel's 100th birthday on November 9, 2018

PART IV
Joseph Popelsky
(1876–1964)

ANCESTRY CHART FOR JOSSEL "JOSEPH" PAPELSKY

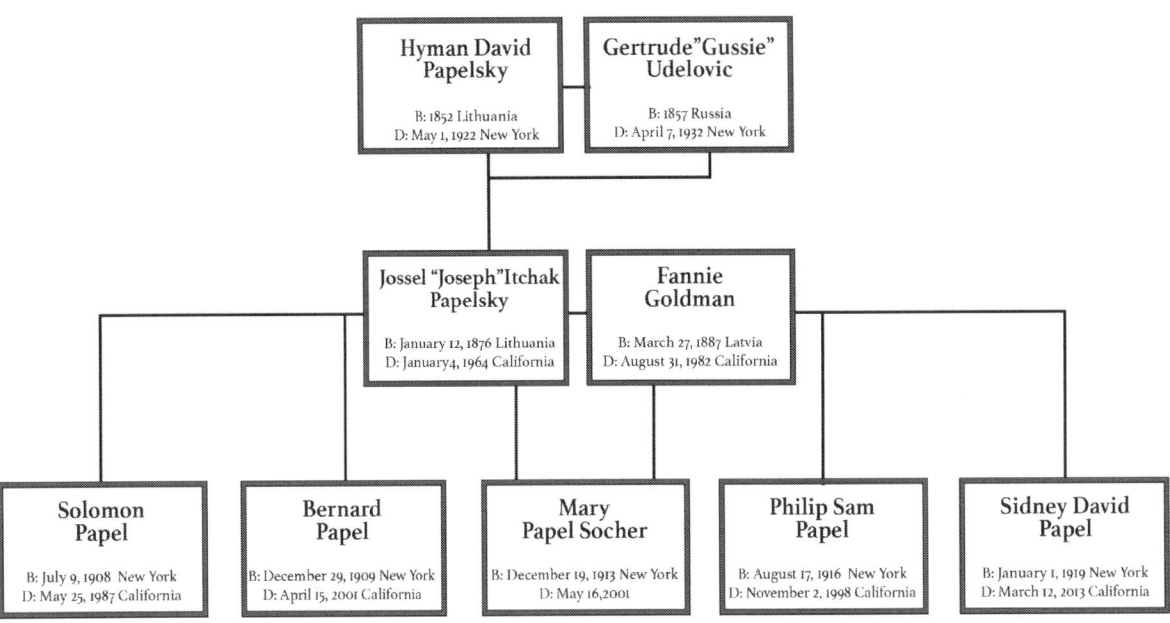

Joseph Popelsky

(1876–1964)

I don't know too much about the childhood of my grandfather, Joseph Popelsky. However, I remember him well from my childhood until his death in 1964. Grandpa Joe was a very kind and quiet man and did not ever share too many details about himself. Even my Dad, who loved him dearly, did not talk about Grandpa Joe's earlier years. I think it was because my Bubbe, Fannie Popelsky, truly dominated his world and he would just roll with the punches.

This what I know. He was born as Jossel (Joseph) Itchak Papelski on January 12, 1876, in Lithuania, which was part of the greater Czarist Russia. His Social Security records listed his birthday as December 17, 1876. I believe that he lived in Lomsa, Lithuania, but was born in Pumpenai (Pompian), Lithuania. He arrived in the United States at Ellis Island at 17 years of age in 1891. The passenger manifest listed his name as Popilski, instead of as Papilski. He took the name of Joseph Popelsky after arriving in America.

We know that Jossel was the son of Haim (Hyman) David Papelsky (1852–1922) and his mother was Gertrude "Gussie" Udelovic (1863–1932). The name of Jossel's grandfather is not currently known, but the married name of his grandmother was Bertha Papelisky.

Jossel (Joseph) was the eldest of six siblings. Yetta (Henrietta) Papilski was born in 1886 in Pumpernai (Pompian), Lithuania. She died in 1930 in Bronx, New York.

Benjamin (Ben) Papilsky was born on November 24, 1888, in Pompian, Lithuania. He was known to be very handsome and was hard of hearing. He was known to be health conscious and was very fit. He lived with his sister, Mary, for many years and was unfortunately killed when he was hit by a car in 1974.

Mary Papilsky Papel was born in Pompian, Lithuania, on December 17, 1890. She settled in New York and lived with my Grandpa Joe. Eventually she moved to New Jersey where she passed away in 1982. I remember Aunt Mary well during her visits to Los Angeles when she would visit my Grandpa Joe and Bubbe. I remember her as a kind and elegant person. She never missed sending me a birthday card and present. I used to love her visits. Coincidentally, her birthday on December 17th is the same as mine. Mary was known as suffragette and labor leader, involved in the formation of the garment union in New York. She married and had a daughter, but very unfortunately both her husband and daughter

Joseph and Fannie Popelsky circa 1939

died very young. She lived in Denver during that time, but after their deaths she returned to live on the East coast.

Lena (Papelsky) Papel was born on June 24, 1893 in Pompian, Lithuania. She died in 1966 in Brooklyn, New York. I do not know too much about her other than she married Dave Aronson in 1925.

Julius (Papelsky) Papel, as the only sibling born in the USA, was born on October 1896 in Brooklyn, New York. He married Regina Greenwald in 1921 in Bronx, New York. I remember Uncle Julius and Aunt Regina very well because they often traveled to California to visit the family. I also remember them from my visits to New York. I know my dad was especially close with Uncle Julius. I also remember Uncle Julius and Aunt Regina made a special trip to California for my Bar Mitzvah in 1955.

My grandfather was a tailor by profession. He always had his thimble with him and would offer to repair any clothes that needed mending. Being a tailor meant he was a modest money provider which I think aggravated my grandmother because she had to do extra things to bring in more money for the family.

Joseph and Fannie Popelsky. New York visit circa 1948

Papel Family Gathering in 1949. Joseph and Fannie Popelsky (seated) with children and spouses: Bernie and Ethyl, Sol and Sonya, Sid, Sophie and Phil, Al and Mary (Socher)

Papel Family Gathering in 1949. Joseph and Fannie Popelsky with children, spouses and grandchildren

I was told that when the family lived in New York, Grandpa Joe was offered a job to be a tailor for the Navy and repair their uniforms. He refused the job because he didn't think it paid enough. However, from the stories told, he didn't realize he would get a lot of referrals from the naval wives and naval community and there would have been a lot more income. Also, this was before the great Depression, so had he accepted the job they would have been in a better financial situation than most working for the government. They would not have moved from New York when they did, which would certainly have been a life changer. However, it was considered to be a major wrong turn in Grandpa Joe's career as a tailor.

I do remember that Grandpa Joe loved his family and enjoyed the family events when we all got together.

Fannie and Joseph dancing at Stanley's Bar Mitzvah 1955

In all the years of his life, I never once saw him angry even when Bubbe was yelling at him. I think in retrospect that even though my grandmother and grandfather seemed to have totally different personalities and ways of viewing the world, that they were solid in their love for family. I think they loved each other, but they just didn't express any emotions to each other.

As I think back on the relationship that I had with my four grandparents, I wish I knew more about my Grandpa Joe. He seems to have been a very kind man, a gentle soul, without a mean bone in his body.

PART V
Fannie Goldman Popelsky
(1887–1982)

ANCESTRY CHART FOR FANNIE GOLDMAN

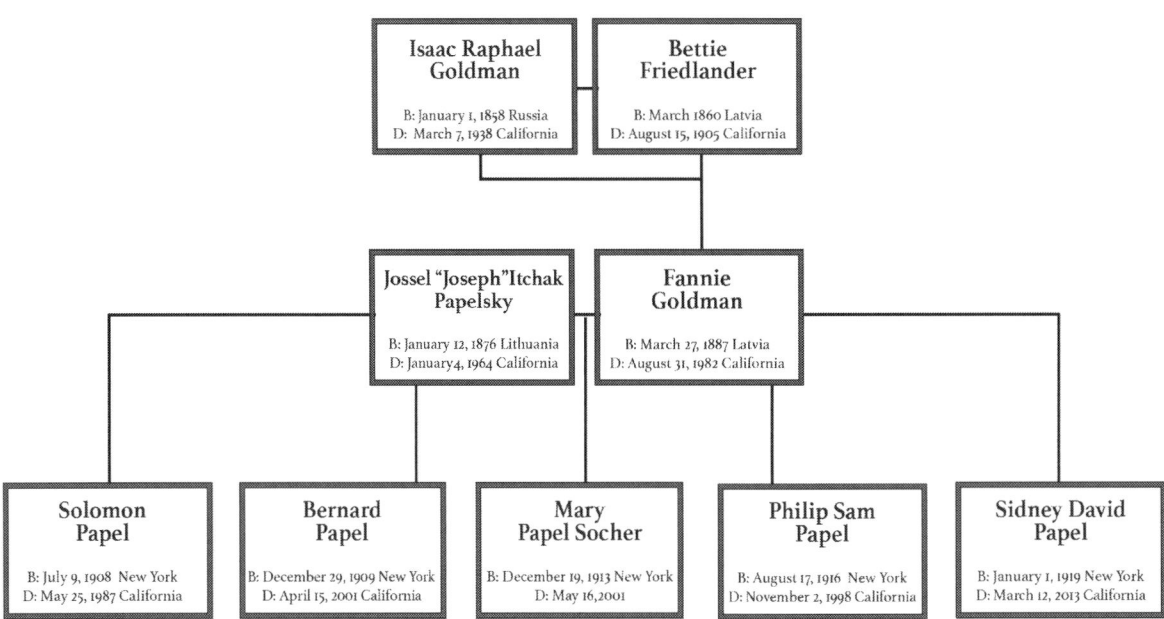

Fannie Goldman Popelsky

(1887–1982)

September 1, 1982

My grandmother was born with the name of Gisa Goldman on March 27, 1887 in Windau (aka Ventspils), Latvia, near the Baltic Sea. From what I understand, she disliked her first name, Gisa, and changed it to Fannie as the family moved from Windau to London when my grandmother was about age 6. Her parents, Isaac Goldman and Bette Friedlander were also born in Windau, Latvia.

There is very little known about Fannie's life in London. If she told any stories about her childhood, they are unfortunately lost through time. However, I do know that they had a hard time in Europe. My great grandfather was a ship painter and shoemaker, and they moved from London to New York City in

Bettie Freelander circa 1894

1895. They then moved to New Haven, Connecticut. I know that Fannie's mother, Bette Goldman, passed away when my grandmother was only 16 years old. My grandmother, Fannie, was the oldest girl and took on the responsibility of the household and raising the younger children. The younger children were Phil 9, Kate 12, and Sam and Rhea were infants. Great Grandpa Isaac remarried again three, four, or five times. I actually have a photography of him where my dad, Phil, who loved his Grandpa Isaac, said he was pictured with his 4th or 5th wife. I know that my grandmother and the other children had a hard time with the different stepmothers, and it was my grandmother Fannie who was maintained the mother-role for all of the siblings.

The Isaac Goldman Family circa 1894. Joe, Bettie, Philip, Harry, Isaac, Katie, Fannie

Isaac Goldman at his Haberdashery

In going through our family archives, I located the wedding invitation of the marriage of Fannie Goldman to Joseph Popilsky on May 20, 1907. It even indicated my grandmother's home address on East 103rd in New York City.

One of my cousins, Barney Young (son of Katy, my grandmother's younger sister), hosted a family reunion of the Goldman family in 1990. He wrote a synopsis of the family which is included in the Appendix. Here is what he had to say about my Fannie Popelsky:

"Fannie was born a little too late for her intended career. She was meant to be the leader of a wagon train crossing the Great Plains. Strong, touch and fierce. She was able to be loving and devoted to those she cared about, but she was rough on those who didn't win her favor. Early in her life she was confronted with the consequences of her mother's death. She had to be a fighter to make it and she survived. The Goldmans used to have great family gatherings at her house out on City Terrace Drive (Boyle Heights, Los Angeles, CA). We called it, "The Farm". There was lots of food, poker playing in the evenings, and a big ball game on the lot next door in the afternoon. I loved to be there. Some the men would get together and form a singing quartet, giving out popular tunes and beer hall songs."

That's good family history and I feel fortunate to know the earlier parts of my Bubbe's life.

I know that while they lived in New York, my grandmother and grandfather were very poor. They had two beds in their tenement housing that slept my grandparents and their five children! The four boys shared a bed, Fannie and Joe another bed, and Mary slept on two chairs back-to-back. They moved from New York to Boyle Heights, Los Angeles, in about 1920 where they were able to buy a small home on City Terrace, which is now part of California's Interstate 10 Freeway.

Fannie Popelsky at Butcher Shop in New York circa 1916

*Isaac Goldman and Leah Goldman (Phil Papel wrote on the back of the picture:
"Leah Goldman was Isaac's 4th or 5th wife. The wedding ring I wear is what he wanted me to have.
He lived with us for years and we were good friends.")*

My first recollections of my Bubbe are very funny. We used to have wonderful family get-togethers with my uncles and aunts, as well as with my cousins. Mom and Dad would tell me we are visiting Grandpa Joe and Bubbe. Well, no one ever told me that "Bubbe" means Grandma in Yiddish. So, I never realized until I was about 7 years old that she was my Grandmother! I thought she was the woman who lived with my Grandpa Joe. After all, they slept in separate bedrooms and they never talked as though they were married and never showed any signs of affection.

As the readers can tell from the earlier details on Bubbe's life, she could be tough. However, she could also be very loving. I knew pretty quickly who was on her good side and who was not. Fortunately, I was one of her very favorites and I liked how she was always so nice to me. In my growing up years, I remember my dad was very good to her and professionally was the most successful of all the siblings. As such, he would primarily be the one who treated my Bubbe and Grandpa to the nicer things in life. Bubbe's younger sister, Rhea, married someone who was also very successful. Her husband, Morris Piltzer, was always very good to my grandparents and we became quite close to them.

When my parents would go on vacations or when my mom accompanied my dad on vacations, it was always Bubbe and Grandpa Joe who took care of us. Actually, I didn't like that very much and could hardly wait for my parents to return home. For one thing, Bubbe was always seemed angry at Grandpa Joe. I think she really loved him, but she was always getting angry at him and yelling at him. Grandpa Joe was hard of hearing and she wasn't patient. He would also miss the toilet sometimes and pee on or around the toilet, and I would hear some choice Yiddish words which I understood weren't very nice.

There are stories about my grandmother's garage which was used for bootlegging during Prohibition. After that, the garage was used as a ceramic factory which outgrew the garage and became a large company which was the start of my dad's career in the giftware industry. The house and the garage on City Terrace hold good memories for me in my childhood years.

Years later my dad helped them buy a home in Alhambra, California, where we continued the family get togethers. After that, when they were aging, my dad rented an apartment for them in the Jewish area of Los Angeles on Hayworth, which was adjacent to Fairfax Avenue. Each time we would visit Bubbe or when she visited us, she would bring her famous baked apples and applesauce. She used to go to the markets on Fairfax and buy their day-old apples, cut out the brown areas, and then make the most delicious applesauce. She never outgrew her roots of poverty, and I remember when we would go to restaurants, I would be so embarrassed when she would take all the sugar packets home with her.

Bubbe had only one daughter who she was very close with since it was the two of them around five men. So, Bubbe told Aunt Mary stories that I never knew. Then Aunt Mary told her daughter, Cheryl Socher-Harwood, all the stories, which Cheryl passed on to me in order to help write the life story of Fannie Popelsky. Here are a few of the quips from Cheryl:

1. Fannie had a serious boyfriend before Joe. I understand he was very successful. I am not sure why the relationship stopped. He later contacted Fannie. Joe got upset and told him he had his chance, and to never contact her again.

2. Aunt Rhea was only 8 or 9 years of age when Fannie and Joe married. Fannie was raising her and Joe didn't mind. Rhea was part of the package. Joe didn't mind and he loved kids. He would have been happy having 10 children but Fannie told him after five kids to "zip it up," meaning to zip up his pants and no more kids. They were very poor and this was before birth control. That is when Joe moved into a separate bedroom.

3. During Prohibition, Fannie got great rent for the Boyle Heights garage. She would also get bottles of booze and sell them.

4. They moved to California because daughter Mary had rheumatic fever for two winters in a row. The doctor told Fannie if they did not move to milder climate that Mary would not make it through another winter.

5. When Fannie was in her eighties, she was walking on Fairfax Blvd. A young man came up to here and said, "your money or your life". She laughed at him and said, "you must be kidding? At my age?" She walked off leaving the would-be robber stunned.

6. On Bubbe's 80th birthday which was given in her honor, everyone was there except Bubbe. It turned out that Sol thought Sid or my Dad were picking her up. Sid thought Sol was picking her up. Dad thought Sid or Sol were picking her up. When they realized the mistake, they rushed out, and you should have seen a very pissed Fannie when she walked into the room!

7. Bubbe used to volunteer for working the election polls. She said she was doing it as a way of repaying the government for giving the women the right to vote. She said she was proud to call herself an American, and she took pride in her ability to talk the dialect of wherever she lived without a Russian, English or New York accent.

8. Grandpa Joe would drive Bubbe nuts by forgetting to turn on his hearing aids. Conversations went like this: Fannie would ask Joe something. He'd say, "What?" She would say it again. He would say, "What?" She would say it louder, and then he would say, "shrina basel" which is Yiddish for "shout softly."

9. Grandpa Joe never did anything domestic in the house. Bubbe would take care of everything.After Grandpa passed, a man from the neighborhood asked her to marry him. Her response was, "What for? I don't need another "alta kocker" (Yiddish for "old man').

10. Bubbe's favorite sayings: " A leopard doesn't change its spots" and "The more I see of people, the more I like dogs." If she liked a man she'd say, "He can put his shoes under my bed anytime." If she didn't like a man, she would call him a "nebish", "schmuck" or "smeckle". You'll have to look that up in a Yiddish dictionary if you want to know the meaning. Basically, Bubbe would say things as she saw it.

11. If she liked you, her eyes would light up when she saw you. I also remember the sparkle in Bubbe's eyes when I would see her.

In the later years, several years after Grandpa Joe died, it was necessary to necessary for Bubbe to move from her apartment to the Jewish Home for the Aged in Reseda. My dad was very active in the organization and also a major contributor. There was no problem getting her a place there although there was a long waiting list. Bubbe's health deteriorated quickly once she moved there. When she passed away, on August 31, 1982, she was at peace with herself and looking back on a difficult but fruitful life. She loved and she was loved.

Here is the Eulogy written by Jack Levin, who was my Dad's best friend:

Fannie Popelsky

Fannie Popelsky at her home in Boyle Heights, Los Angeles CA in 1936

Telling about Fannie Popelsky is somewhat like trying to explain in English a Yiddish story. It loses something in the translation. And when we talk of losing something, we realize that we have lost a one in a million, a unique and courageous woman.

Although what I know of Fannie first 60 years, I learned from Phil, I did have the privilege of insuring her for the last 36 years of her life. We all have known mothers that were loved by their children and grandchildren; less common was Fannie who was not only dearly, but also greatly admired and respected. I know of and had expressed many of Fannie's admirable qualities. She was strong, compassionate, fair, and wise. Independent and proud and fiercely protective of her family and a good judge of character.

She had a keen dry sense of humor was very outspoken. What was on her mind was on her lips. The combinations sometimes got her into hot water. She was very resourceful as was demonstrative by one of my favorite stories about Fannie that Phil likes to tell.

When the Popelsky family lived in City Terrace, they had a garage, but didn't dream of having a car to put in it. So, Fannie rented the garage to a man for a few dollars a month. Later when she realized that instead of using the garage to park a car, he was using it as a bootlegger warehouse. She tripled the rent and got it.

Fannie, as you know, looked like Golda Meir and she loved to talk about how people would stop her on the street and ask her in fact she was the famous and beloved Golda. I believed, as did others, that Fannie and Golda shared many admirable qualities.

Those of you who have read "World of Our Fathers" will recognize Fannie Popelsky throughout its pages. From the Russian Shtetl, her family dreaming of America, to the ordeal of the crossing in steerage onto Ellis Island, the shock of the new world, the sweat shops, scrubbing the halls and stairways of the tenement in Brooklyn where they lived in order to get a reduction in the rent. Reading the Yiddish dailies when they cost a penny. The Catskills, the Yiddish theater with Boris Thomashefsky and Bertha Kalish. Moving west because her daughter, Mary, had asthma and settling in City Terrance. The struggle just to survive, let alone educate the children.

Fannie's fantastic capacity for work first trying to keep the family together. You will recognize in those pages, Fannie, and realize that she is among the very last to have lived and successfully survived the experiences of eastern European Jewish immigrants. The only way to know is to read about it.

It is not my purpose here today to glorify Fannie, she would not like that. Rather I honor her for the unique and unforgettable woman that she was. A woman who made the most of her place in history. She will truly be missed.

With love, respect and admiration.
Jack Levin

Fannie Popelsky's 80th Birthday.
Sol, Sidney, Phil and Mary in 1967

Fannie Popelsky on cover for
Papel Imports first catalogue in 1976

PART VI
Mihaly ("Mike") Roth
(1876–1948)

ANCESTRY CHART
FOR
MIHALY "MICHAEL" ROTH

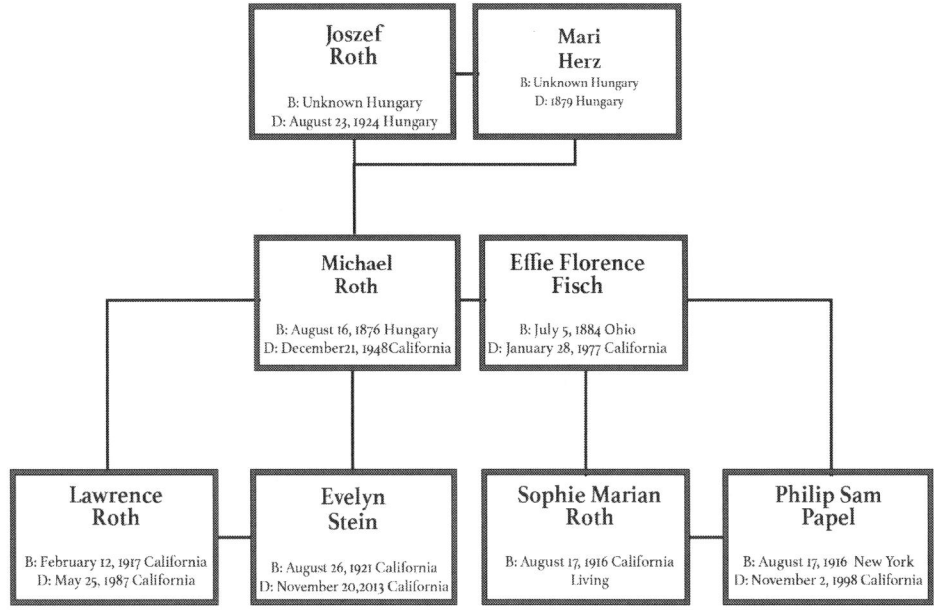

CHAPTER 1

Mihaly "Mike" Roth
Childhood Memories (1876–1948)

The Life of Mike Roth
by Sophie Papel

My father, Mike Roth, was born in 1876 in Kovacsvagas, a little Hungarian village. In this town there was only one school and two houses of worship: one Christian and one Jewish. The population consisted mostly of peasant farmers who raised their own cattle, wheat, potatoes, and vegetables. My father was one from a family of 10 children and he happened to be the ninth child. His mother died when he was a child of three, so that he has no recollection of her. There was never a picture taken of his mother, so that he does not even know what she looked like.

My grandfather was a very hard-working man in his younger days. He was Kovacsvagas' butcher, a grocer, and a saloonkeeper. He was also a farmer and a synagogue member. The family consisted of four girls and six boys, all of whom grew up, married, and raised families. Seven of the children are still living.

After his mother died, Mike's father married again but there were no children from the second marriage. My step-grandmother was also a hard-working woman and she was very good to all the children, but there was always the feeling that she was not their own mother. Once each week, she would get up at two o'clock in the morning and bake the bread for a week's supply. She also made the family clothes by hand and even cut each child's hair when needed.

Mike's stepmother would never spank or punish any of the children but if the children would do something wrong, she would go to their father and he would do the punishing. My father's recollection is that he was the child who got the most spankings from his father because he was quite afraid of him and was jealous of his youngest brother who seemed to be the pet. In spite of the fact that he was very strict with his children, at times Mike's father was very kind and on holidays gathered the children all about him and enjoyed playing games with them.

One incident that stands out in my father's mind was the time when he was a small child. He, his younger brother, and another little boy went to the river to go bathing. After bathing, he persuaded them to walk several miles to the next town to visit their grandmother. When they got there, they were very tired; and it was already dark. Their grandmother, not knowing how to send them home, gave them their dinner and put them to bed. On the following morning, she gave them a good breakfast, and they went out in the garden, played, and climbed apple trees. Many branches were broken, and many green apples were eaten.

It happened that a sister of the boys was sent out looking for them and when she saw them playing and having a good time, she thanked my father's grandmother for taking care of them and took all three of the small boys back home. My father's parents were very much worried about them because they thought they might have drowned in the river. They did not get a wink of sleep that night. My father got the biggest and hardest spanking he ever got in his life and I guess that that is the reason he remembers this incident and will never forget it.

Mike Roth. Los Angeles, CA circa 1910

CHAPTER 2

MIHALY "MIKE" ROTH
SCHOOL DAYS (1876–1948)

When my father was old enough to go to school, his father hired a young man to serve as schoolteacher. The first day, my father played hooky. The second day he went to school, which was in a dilapidated building, and beat his teacher. Mike's father was compelled to hire an older and stronger teacher, whom he instructed to punish my father if he did not mind or if failed to study.

Each student was compelled to take up reading, writing, arithmetic, and three languages. Those, which my father took, were Hebrew, Hungarian and German.

Different teachers were hired from year to year and received very little pay for each child. The teacher would board with the families of the different children on different days. Once they had a teacher who had a habit of giving the students a weekly lesson in translation. At the end of the week for each mistake the student received a sound thrashing.

After putting up with this for several weeks my father filled his pockets with stones. He went through his regular lesson with the usual amount of errors. The teacher was about to thrash Mike's younger brother when my father got up from his bench with a stone in his hand and threatened his teacher that if he touched his brother the teacher would have a broken head. The teacher was shocked and did not touch Mike's brother but told Mike that he would tell his father what Mike had done. My father went home and confessed to his stepmother. Acting as an intermediary she told her husband and they both agreed that he was right. My father did not get a spanking from his father, and the teacher never gave any more severe spankings or punishments.

The children in the family all had to do their share of work from the time they were old enough to do so. My father's first duty was to see that wood was always in the house for heating and cooking. When he was older, he had to chop his share of wood, help clean the stable, clean the cows, drive the flies away while the cows were being milked, help dig up potatoes and drive the geese to the pasture.

The farm consisted of two horses, two dogs, two cats, two cows, calves, about 100 chickens, 50 ducks and 30 geese. There was always plenty of work to do on a farm, but a country boy can also have a good time, playing in the haystacks and with the animals, and having a lot of fun raising a calf and watching it grow. It was a pet to the children.

At the age of 20, my father's oldest brother was taken into the army. This caused his father much grief and worry and a large sum of money. When the time approached to take his second son into the army, he sent him to the United States. His father had learned a lesson. When the rest of the boys reached 13 years of age, they had to leave home, learn some profession or trade, and start life for themselves. The girls stayed home until they got married. Only two sisters and one brother stayed in the same town where they were born.

CHAPTER 3

MIHALY "MIKE" ROTH
TROUBLESOME DAYS (1876–1948)

When Mike was 13 years old, his father took him to the closest city and left him there at a cobbler's shop as an apprentice. After he had been away from home for a week, one of his sisters came to visit him. When he saw her, he began to cry and insisted on going home with her. His father then took him to another village much farther away where he could not get home as easily and left him with the understanding that he was to learn how to make boots and shoes. However, instead of teaching him to make boots and shoes, the man made an errand boy of him. He made him clean the shop, make beds, shine shoes, deliver shoes, go out and buy food for breakfast, lunch and supper for the men, and chop wood.

The men worked from 6 a.m. to midnight, so my father had very little time to learn anything about making shoes. When his time was up, all he knew was a little repair work—he knew he could not make a living, so he went home.

His father again found a place where he could learn more for his room and board. This time, he made a contract with a cobbler for a term of three years. If this contract was broken, his father would have had to pay a large sum of money. Although in this place he also did not learn much about making shoes and he did not like what work there was, he stayed the full three years and when the contract was up, he gladly went home.

After he had been home for a few days, his father took him to a piece of land he had bought cheap. This land was on a side of a mountain. When it rained, the water washed some of the soil away and left a big hole in the center of the field, which had to be refilled before it could be cultivated. Mike's father filled a basket with heavy stones which my father lifted, carried, and dumped into the bottom of the hole. This was going on for quite some time until he realized that this was very hard work. My father started to cry. When his father discovered it, he gave him a good lecture, telling him he would never be a good farmer and he might as well understand right then and there that he better stick to his trade for his own good.

The next day, my dad's father gave him a small number of *forints*, the Hungarian national currency. He said to my dad, "My boy, you have your trade. Go where your eyes take you. Hustle and make a living." His stepmother packed him a lunch. My father took his few belongings and a few tools and left home in the rainy weather crying. He was 16 years then and determined not to go home until he was successful. This was really the making of my father, Mike, and he did not see his father again for four years.

CHAPTER 4

MIHALY "MIKE" ROTH
IN BUDAPEST (1876–1948)

Leaving the small village in Hungary, my father started out for the capital, Budapest, where his father's brother lived. This was a distance of about fifty miles. He had only the money his father had given him, so he walked partway and took the train partway, until he reached a town in which an uncle lived and where his younger brother worked. He stayed with his brother overnight. In the morning, his uncle gave him more money and he continued on his way to Budapest. After two days, he arrived in Budapest, very tired and dirty. With the help of a man to whom he paid his last *krajczár*, he finally found his uncle.

His uncle was very glad to see him. He took him into the house, had him bathe and clean up, and after a good dinner, they talked about the future. It was decided that my father was to continue the trade his father had picked for him, and that he was to live with his uncle. Although he hated the cobbler trader, he continued it for three more years. In these three years, he managed to save up about $400 and to keep himself well clothed.

He and his uncle had another talk. His uncle saw how dissatisfied he was, so he concluded that he had better try something else. My father secured a position in a publishing house. His duties were to collect money for advertising, to mail out the magazines to subscribers, and to deliver the magazine to stores. He enjoyed the work very much and was very well liked by his employer.

It was now almost four years that he had been away from home. He told his employer that he would like to visit his father and spend the Pesach holiday at home. He was given a week's vacation. His father was very happy to see him as were the rest of his family and he had a very good time on this visit. Although he did not know it, this was the last time he was to see his father and birthplace.

He returned to Budapest and continued to work for the publishing house and advanced quite rapidly.

Two of his older brothers were already living in Los Angeles. They were both in business there and were very successful. He wrote them letters telling them that he had saved up about $500 and that he also would like to leave for the United States. They replied that they were sending money to Germany covering transportation for him and his younger brother to come to Los Angeles.

He was very happy and made arrangements to meet his brother in Germany. Together, they left the old country behind them and start out anew in a strange land.

CHAPTER 5

MIHALY "MIKE" ROTH
IN AMERICA (1876–1948)

My father left Budapest on August 16, 1896, and stayed in Germany for about a month until his younger brother arrived there. The steamer left for the United States at eight o'clock in the morning. Neither boy had ever been on a boat before, and the first night they both got very seasick. This did not last very long, however, and when they got used to the sea both thought the trip was very wonderful. It took eight days to reach New York. They stayed in New York for eight days where they visited with different relatives and then left for Los Angeles.

Just before they reached Los Angeles, their oldest brother got on the train at Riverside Station. As they were not expecting anyone on the train to meet them, they were very much delighted. Their other brother was waiting at the depot to meet them. It was about 15 years since my father had seen one of his brothers and about 10 years since he had seen his other brother, so they had a very happy reunion.

My father started to work for one of his brothers who was in the cigar business. It took a great deal of time to learn the name of the different cigars and their prices. My father did not know one word of English when he came to the United States. He went to night school and studied English and many other subjects to help in the future. He and his younger brother lived together in one room.

My father's oldest brother married shortly after he arrived. At his brother's wedding, my father celebrated and learned a good lesson. Friends filled his glass with white and red wine until my father was drunk. He was very sick all night and made up his mind that such foolishness would never happen to him again. I am proud to say that he has lived up to that resolution and has never got drunk since that one time when he was tricked into it.

After working for his brother for four years, my father left him and started a little business of his own. He worked long hours and made more money than when he worked for his brother. After 16 months, he sold this business at a profit. He then bought another cigar stand, which was also a success to such an extent that Mike was able to employ a man to help him. My father kept this business for five years until the building where the cigar shop was located was torn down.

Mike Roth. 1st Cigar Store in Los Angeles, CA circa 1912

Mike Roth. Sundries Store in Los Angeles, CA circa 1914

My father next bought a grocery, fruit and cigar store. The location was very good, on Seventh Street near Broadway in Los Angeles, and he did very well. However, the landlord had fooled my father, for in about six months he got a notice to move as the building was to be torn down. He had to sell his merchandise at a loss.

Right here, I would like to quote from an article, which appeared in a Los Angeles newspaper about four years after my father arrived in the United States:

"The above portraits are of the four Roth brothers engaged in business in this city. They are all natives of Hungary and are the only members of their immediate family in the country, but they are as True Americans as Los Angeles can boast of. The father of these young men is now 62 years of age and resides in Hungary. One brother resides with his father and is an officer in the Hungarian army. Two sisters are married and lived in the Fatherland."

It then goes on tell about each brother in particular, but I will only quote what it says about my father Mike:

"The third brother is Mike Roth, 24 years of age. He arrived in Los Angeles in 1896. He is engaged in the cigar business at 400 South Main Street and is, as the other members of the group, eminently successful. He is unmarried."

After my father gave up on the grocery business, he had some cigars and tobacco on hand. He sold this leftover stock to cigar stands at a profit, and this gave him the idea to go into the wholesale cigar and tobacco business. He managed this wholesale business for a number of years and had a very large trade making quite a profit. He invested money in real estate. Some, he sold at a profit and some he still has. He also invested in mining and oil stocks, but he lost whatever he invested that way.

PART VII
Effie Fisch Roth
(1884–1977)

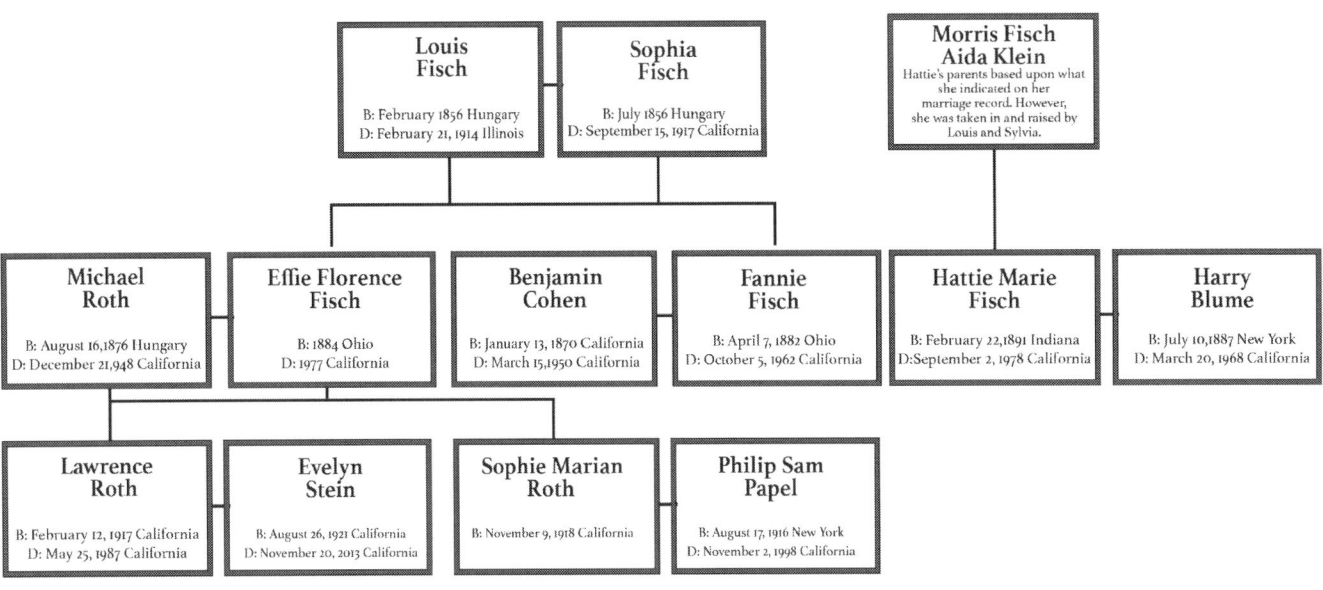

Effie Fisch Roth

(1884–1977)

On July 5, 1877, Effie Florence Fisch was born on in Cincinnati, Ohio, to Louis Fisch and Sophie Fisch. Louis and Sophie were first cousins who were both from Hungary. When young, they knew each other in Hungary but were married in America.

Louis Fisch was considered to be the black sheep of his family. He was sent alone to the United States in 1876 by his father, Ignatz, hoping that he would find success in the new world. Ignatz Fisch's brother was Abraham Fisch, the father of Sophie Fisch. Thus, Louis and Sophie not only shared the same last name before marriage, they were first cousins.

Louis and Sophie had three daughters: Fannie, Effie, and Hattie (Footnote 1). Fannie was born in Cincinnati, Ohio, in April 1883, and Effie was born there in July 1884. Hattie was born in Indiana in February 1888.

The family eventually moved from Cincinnati, Ohio, to Chicago, Illinois. The 1900 census lists Louis Fisch as an immigrant while stating that he was a clerk by occupation. He was whispered in family circles as being a gambler and a drinker.

Sophie Fisch was a follower of early woman's suffrage movement pioneer Jane Addams. Addams established the Settlement House Movement in the United States and was the second woman to win a Nobel Peace Prize. She also co-founded the Hull House, a famous settlement house run by intellectual women that afforded social and educational gatherings for newly resettled European immigrants and working-class residents in Chicago. Addams influenced Sophie Fisch to move to Los Angeles with her three daughters, which concurrently led to the separation from her husband, Louis Fisch. Their move from Chicago to Los Angeles is believed to have occurred sometime around 1912.

Jane Addams is well known in USA history as one of the first leaders of women's suffrage. There was a lot of talk at the time of Jane Addams taking a liking to Sophie Fisch and her three daughters, as well as in having a major influence in encouraging the separation from Louis. She had a positive influence in the three sisters each receiving a higher education and becoming very independent reformed thinkers. Jane Addams was known to be a lesbian with a partner although that was not why Sophie Fisch left Louis Fisch. Sophie Fisch remained in contact with Louis over the years. When Louis became ill, she was by his side and arranged for his tombstone and burial at Chicago's Forest Home cemetery (known today as Waldheim Jewish Cemetery) at Forest Park, Illinois in 1914.

Dinner Party with Effie Fisch and Hattie Fisch in los Angeles, CA circa 1914

Mike Roth Wedding 1916

All three of Sophie's daughters obtained a post-secondary education with Fannie and Hattie graduating from college while Effie went to college but finished her education at secretarial school to become a stenographer. Addams helped Effie land a job as a secretary for a railroad company in Los Angeles by writing an impressive letter of recommendation. Sophie Fisch and her daughters were all progressive in women's rights at that time and were among the relatively few women who were given the opportunity to graduate from college during this era.

Effie met her future husband Mike Roth in 1915. Mike, a Hungarian immigrant, came to the United States searching for new opportunities when he was twenty years old. Effie and Mike were introduced through his uncle Shamu Perluss and wife Rosie. Uncle Shamu had met Effie at a B'nai B'rith function and thought she would be a wonderful lady for his nephew. Effie and Mike married on March 9, 1916 and they went on their honeymoon to San Diego.

Mike bought a house on 1545 Third Avenue near Arlington for their residence. Mike owned a cigar store

Roth Family. Larry, Mike, Sophie and Effie in 1919

in Los Angeles through the help of his brother, Kelly Roth, who immigrated earlier than Mike. He later owned a grocery store in Watts that he rented out along with vacant lots in Hemet that provided income for them. Although Effie retired from her secretarial job after getting married, she still took care of financial matters such as taking care of the leases at the grocery stores. She was very businesslike and paid the bills at home.

On February 12, 1917, Effie gave birth to her first child, Larry. The following year, her daughter Sophie Marian Roth was born on November 9, 1918. Effie was a loving mother who meticulously watched over her children. Sophie wanted a puppy or a kitten, a notion that Effie did not agree with, as she feared that her daughter could get sick from the diseases that she believed the animals carried. Still, she understood when a dog on the beach jumped on three-year old Sophie licking her face and scaring her, quipping that the dog was being playful and did not mean any harm. She did not play with the kids as much as her husband did as she was busy doing her household chores.

Effie's daughter, Sophie Roth, was the good girl who rarely got into trouble. However, once when Sophie was four years old and they were at the beach, Effie gave her a nickel to purchase an ice cream cone. Sophie got lost on the pier and could not find her mother. Fortunately, a kind police officer led her back to her parents at a dry goods store on the Ocean Front.

Effie took her daughter to kindergarten when she was about five years old and stayed with her the entire first day. However, the second day, Effie was about to leave Sophie behind with the rest of the class, but she started to cry. Effie said that Sophie did not have to stay in class if she chose not to but gave her a stern lecture at home about the importance of going to school by herself. She told Sophie that she would take Sophie back to school when she was ready. After a month, Sophie was finally ready to attend classes and Effie took her back to school.

On the other hand, Larry tended to be rambunctious as a youngster and often got into trouble. Later he outgrew the mischievous stage and became an Eagle Scott, and a star athlete in many sports and became a champion shot-put thrower.

Effie was extremely close to her sisters Hattie and Fannie. She would often bring her daughter Sophie to visit them. Fannie was married to Ben Cohen and had a daughter Marian. Hattie divorced her husband and had a daughter Stephanie. The sisters and their kids would go on weeklong vacations during the summer to the beach or to Catalina Island, while their husbands stayed at home.

One of the more adventurous vacations occurred in 1923. Effie and her sister Hattie took their kids up to Seven Oaks intending to have a nice two- or three-week holiday. They stayed in two log cabins, which had an abundance of spiders to the dismay of everyone. Additionally, they went to the cow stables to drink some fresh milk, but it was warm and had a repulsive taste. After two days, they had enough and went up to Big Bear Lake where they had a wonderful time staying in nice accommodations, having an excellent culinary experience and discovering interesting sites such as the Silver Fox farm and the Lucky Baldwin Gold Mine They also took a boat ride on Big Bear Lake.

Every Sunday, the Roth family would take the streetcar to Ocean Park Beach or Venice Beach where they spent the entire day.

Effie was a colorful woman who loved to quack idioms like "It's raining cats and dogs; I just stepped in a poodle." She sang to her kids a humorous song with the lyrics, "After the Ball was over, Lilly took out her glass eye, took her false teeth in the corner."

Roth Family and Relatives ... Venice Beach circa 1927

She cooked American dishes such as meatloaf for her family and raised her kids to observe American traditions like Christmas and Thanksgiving. She used to fill the Christmas stockings of her children with little treats such as fruits. Although she was a proud Jew and never had a tree in her house, she wanted her kids to feel American and encouraged them to celebrate Christmas with their neighbor families.

Effie proudly observed the Jewish holidays spending a lot of time cooking for Passover Seders. She sent her kids to Sunday school at the B'nai B'rith on Wilshire Blvd. Sophie got confirmed when she was 15 years old. Effie brought her a beautiful dress for the occasion as Sophie spoke in front of the Temple. She also hosted a nice party for her daughter afterwards.

The Great Depression, which began in October 1929, hit the family hard. Mike lost $26,000 in the stock market, which was a good sum of money back then. In addition, the Roth family nearly lost their home due to foreclosure because Mike could not afford to make mortgage payments on the house. Effie, the perceptive businesswoman, went to the bank and pleaded with them to not kick her family out of the home, citing the harsh economic conditions. The bank relented and they remained in the Third Avenue home. Eventually, the mortgage on the house was paid off. Effie and her family were fortunate compared to other families during the Depression, as they were still able to live comfortably.

Mike retired around 1934 while the kids matured into high school students. Effie was never worried about Sophie, who was always seemingly on a date and was quite popular. Effie was proud to see her two children get married. Larry married Evie Stein while Sophie tied the knot with Phil Papel. Effie quickly grew to appreciate Phil after Sophie's 20th birthday

Roth Family and Stephanie Blume (front left)
3rd Avenue Los Angeles, CA circa 1928

Mike and Effie Roth circa early 1930's

party, and he stayed after everyone left and cleaned the whole house. Effie fell in love with him for his kindness, and she knew he was a nice person.

The 1940's marked both happiness and sadness for Effie. She had four grandchildren born during the decade beginning with Sophie's son Stanley Louis Papel in 1942, followed by Larry's daughter Geraldine (Geri) Roth the following year. Sophie's daughter Arlene was born in 1947 followed by her last grandchild, Larry's son, Marc, in 1949. However, it also was the decline of her husband Mike who had suffered a stroke while playing pinochle with her at the beginning of the decade. Although he was able to recover, he struggled hearing conversations and had to use a cane. He fought diabetes for the remainder of his life and passed away in 1948.

During World War II with Phil in the Navy, Sophie and her newborn son Stan moved back into Effie's 3rd Avenue house, where Effie and Mike helped raise their new grandson while Phil served in the Navy. They spent three years living with Sophie's parents.

Seated Left to Right: Effie Roth, Mike Roth, Kelly Roth, Rosie (Roth) Weinstock, Abe Roth (Referee), Ethyl Roth, Max Roth.

Standing Left to Right: Phil Papel, Sophie (Roth) Papel, Evie Roth, Larry Roth, Minnie Roth, Clarence Roth, Isidor Roth, Charlene Roth (2nd wife to Isidor), Judge Lester Roth, Gertrude Roth, Elenor Roth (daughter of Lester Roth), man in the background is possibly Rudy Winkler, Jack Roth, Jennie Roth (older lady), Marian Roth.

Notes: The only Roth brother that is missing from the photograph is Sam Roth. Rosie Weinstock is the sister to the Roth brothers.

Roth Family circa 1937 *Effie and Mike Roth at Sophie and Phil's wedding on May 21, 1939*

After Mike passed way in 1948, Effie lived with Hattie together in a 3-bedroom home on 3rd Avenue. Hattie was a social worker and the job kept her quite busy, thus Effie cleaned the house, cooked, and had more time to spend with the kids. They used to go vacations together to places such as Palm Springs. When Fannie's husband passed away, she moved in with Effie's family. Hattie had a car and took her older sister to the market, doctor, and they enjoyed going out to dinner.

When Phil was away on business, Sophie would often invite her mother, Effie, which she welcomed, since she loved to be with her grandkids. Stan had a very close and special relationship with Effie, having lived the first three years of his life with her. She took him on the streetcar downtown to the bank where she had a vault. She invested savings bonds for Stan and her other grandchildren. Although she may have seemed mysterious to Stan, guarding her age and rattling in her memorable idioms, he admired her and named his second child Evan after her when she was still alive.

Effie collected anything with a fish on it because her surname was Fisch. She had plates, utensils with fish engraved on it, and her family would give her "fish" gifts. When Phil was on a business trip, he had a very modern plate made in Italy with a beautiful picture of fish.

In the 1960's, the three sister's home on Third Avenue home was broken into at night. Hattie was talking on the phone to her daughter Stephanie and they heard something in the front bedroom. Effie could see through the mirror that there was a man who got in the middle bedroom window, and she yelled at him to get out. Fortunately he ran away.

The Three Sisters. Fannie Cohen, Hattie Blume, Effie Roth circ eary 1930's

Roth Family and Relatives. Venice Beach 1941

Sophie told Hattie and Ettie it was not safe anymore to live in the area anymore. She had them move to an apartment in West Los Angeles, close to Sophie and Stephanie. They had lived in that house for 50 years. Larry and Sophie had to go through things, which was a big job. Effie got shingles in her 80's while moving. She lived the last ten years of her life there. She had to walk with a walker, but she was able to get around. She helped make dinner with Hattie, and she would set the table. The two sisters would coordinate tasks. When Hattie passed away, Sophie took care of her.

In 1976, Effie had heart failure, and they had to send her to a convalescent home near Sophie and Larry. Sophie went there every day. Effie's mind was very sharp and she was alert until the end. The only day Sophie did not come on time was on Tuesday when she was playing Mahjong. Sophie went to visit Effie right after her game concluded and Effie knew why Sophie was tardy. Effie spent the final two months of her life there. She lost her ability to speak at the end and squeezed both Stan's and Sophie's fingers to say goodbye. She passed away very quietly on January 28, 1977.

Note: At the time of the writing of this biography in 2009, it was always believed that the "three sisters" were sisters. Their children and grandchildren never knew anything different. Through Ancestory.com it was learned that Hattie Fisch was really not a sister! It turned out that Sophie's father, Abraham, had a brother by the name of Moritz. Moritz lived in Los Angeles with his wife Bertha.

Bertha passed away and Moritz had a daughter, Hattie, with another woman whom he did not marry. Moritz asked that Sophie and Louis raise Hattie as their daughter. Thus, Hattie was actually a step-first cousin to Fannie and Effie who were true sisters. The evidence was on Hattie's marriage license to Harry Blume, where she listed the names of her biological mother and father.

*Great Great Grandfather Aaron Shajie Fisch.
B. 1784, D. 1857*

Great Grandfather Louis Fisch. B. 1856, D. 1914

*Great Grandmother Sophia Fisch.
B. 1856, D. 1917*

*Great Grandmother Sophia Fisch.
B. 1856, D. 1917*

Great Grandfather Joszef Roth with 3rd Wife (unknown name). B. circa 1824, D. 1924

APPENDICES

Jacob Hyman Papilsky (Yiddish Name: Yankel Chaim) and Sarah Super.
Wedding in Germiston, South Africa in 1904

"What's in a Name?"

Do you know the most common question I get about the last name 'Papel'? It's "Did you know your last name means 'Paper' in Spanish?" Since it seems that I have heard the question more than a thousand times, I often am tempted to say, "Oh, really? I never knew that!"

However, I wanted to find out where the name really came from. Here is the information I have received from my cousin, Ron Lapid, in Israel, who keeps track of the exact spellings of the family name. In the "old country" the official name was written in Cyrillic. When it was written in Latin letters on the passport or Ship Embarkation list, all kinds of options opened themselves -especially with the vowels. For the vowel between the first "P" and the second "P" we have examples of "a", "i" and "o". Then between the "p" and "l" we have examples of "e", "i" and "u". And the last letter was sometimes written "y" or "i". And sometimes the "l" was omitted.

This gives us at least a dozen options of writing the name, though they all referred to the same family: Papilsky, Pipilsky, Popilsky, Papelsky, Papulsky, Papisky, Papilski, Pipilski, Popilski, Popelsky, Papelski, Papulski, Papiski.

Back in the 1700's many Europeans had only first names. Later it became a law in Czarist Russia that people must have first and last names. Many people at that time chose their profession such as Taylor (from Tailor), Smith (from Goldsmith), Chamberlin (from owner of sleeping chambers), Miller, and so on. Other people chose from their father's name, such as Johnson, Richardson, etc. However, many people took the locale in which they were living at the time. Hence, it is entirely possible that an ancestor from a village or small town in Latvia or Lithuania chose names similar to or the same as their town. In the case of my ancestors, they lived near the village of Papilys, which sounds very much like "Papilsky."

I was also able to track from a source, my friend and associate Rick Scott, that in the year 2020 there are about 100 households with the last name Papel. Most are in the USA (52 families), followed by France (21) and Canada (11). Australia and Great Britain have a few families, and there is even one in Germany. If these people are all related, I have no idea. I have met cousins with the last name "Papilsky," who live in South Africa. (See photo.)

As I inquired further about the name Papel, an online search revealed that there is a tribe in Guinea Bissau that numbers 115,000 according to a 2012 estimate. The Papels (also called Pepels) are engaged in hunting and agriculture. I think I can say with 100% certainty that this is a coincidence and not connected with the origin of our family from Lithuania.

I hope that someday one of my grandchildren or great grandchildren (not born yet) will be interested enough to find out more about our family history and the source of their family name.

Index of Names

(p) photo only

A
Addams, Jane
Allenberg, John
Anka, Paul

B
Balzer, Robert Lawrence
Bellah, Geoffrey
Berrie, Angelica
Berrie, Russ
Bernstein, Dr. Robert
Blume, Hattie Fisch
Brown, David

C
Carter, Randy
Chamberlain, Katie
Chamberlain, Kerrie
Chamberlain, Liz
Chamberlain, Steven Kent
Cohen, Fannie Roth
Cooper, Toby

D
Danciart, Frank
Danciart, Wanda
Disney, Walt
Donley, Ruth
Duck, Donald

E
Edwards, Blake

F
Fisch, Aaron Shajie *(p)*
Fisch, Abraham
Fisch, Bertha
Fisch, Ignatz
Fisch, Louis
Fisch, Moritz
Fisch, Sophie

Flavia
Flicker, Ira
Freedman, Jim
Friedlander, Bette

G
Ganz, Al
Gauthier, Mark
Gelfand, Josh
Gilhooley, Jim
Ginsberg, Ira
Gold, Aileen Iona
Goldfeder, Howard
Goldman, Harry *(p)*
Goldman, Isaac *(p)*
Goldman, Joe *(p)*
Goldman, Kate
Goldman, Leah *(p)*
Goldman, Philip
Goldman, Sam

H
Hall, Pamela
Harwood, Cheryl Socher
Hayashi, Kazuo
Highland, Chuck
Himovitz, Earl
Himovitz, Elaine
Himovitz, Fred

I
Islas, Jose
Iwamoto, Mack

J
Jacobson, Geri Roth
Jones, David

K
Kamins, Bernie
Kamins, Marni

Kamins, Piper
Kamins, Sue
Katz, Barbara
Kipper, Nancy
Kipper, Steve
Koopersmith, Arnold
Koopersmith, Nancy Rand

L
Lapid, Ron
Leff, Bob
Leff, Carole
Leff, Stephanie Blume
Lesser, Robin
Levin, Jack
Lewis, Jo
Levin, Shiffra
Lipton, Max
Lipton, Yona
Lynn, Gail
Lynn, Roland

M
Mack, Jean
Mason, Dave
Matsui, Shigeru
McDougal, Denis
Miller, Adele
Miller, Joseph
Miller, Leo
Miyake, Bessie "Frank"
Moscot, Gregg
Moscot, Joel
Moscot, Lily Josephine
Moscot, Melissa Papel
Moscot, Oliver Harrison
Moscot, Theodora

N
Niven, David

O

P

Papel, Bernard
Papel, Dara Michele
Papel, Deborah Roseman
Papel, Ethyl
Papel, Evan Todd
Papel, Geraldine *(p)*
Papel, Jerry *(p)*
Papel, Joe Aaron
Papel, Julius
Papel, Lena
Papel, Mark *(p)*
Papel, Phil
Papel, Phinley Jacob
Papel, Regina Greenwald
Papel, Rochelle
Papel, Sidney
Papel, Sol
Papel, Sonya *(p)*
Papel, Sophie
Papel, Stanley Louis
Papelsky, Bertha
Papelsky, Haim David
Papilsky, Benjamin
Papilsky, Jacob Hyman *(p)*
Pelkowitz, Keren Simon
Perluss, Rosie
Perluss, Shamu
Phillips, Blake
Piltzer, Morris
Piltzer, Rhea Goldman
Pollokoff, Leo
Popelsky, Fannie Goldman
Popelsky, Joseph

Q

R

Roseman, Izzy
Roseman, Pam
Roseman, Nev
Roseman, Rita
Roth, Abe *(p)*
Roth, Charlene *(p)*
Roth, Clarence *(p)*
Roth, Effie Fisch
Roth, Eleanor *(p)*
Roth, Evie *(p)*
Roth, Gertrude *(p)*
Roth, Isidor *(p)*
Roth, Jack *(p)*
Roth, Jennie *(p)*
Roth, Joszef *(p)*
Roth, Kelly
Roth, Larry
Roth, Leah *(p)*
Roth, Lester *(p)*
Roth, Marc
Roth, Marian *(p)*
Roth Mike
Roth, Minnie *(p)*
Rrig, Phil
Ruggles, Charles

S

Saklad, Dick
Sanders, Dr. Gerald
Scott, Rick
Seigel, Barry
Seigel, Dale Miller
Sellers, Peter
Siegel, Gary
Silver, Mary Papelsky
Silverman, Mike
Simon, Chloe
Sinatra, Frank
Slater, Arlene Papel
Slater, Brad
Slater, Jay
Slater, Kim
Socher, Al *(p)*
Socher, Barry *(p)*
Socher, Mary Papel
Starr, Barbara
Sulzberger, Henry
Super, Sarah *(p)*

T

Takeshi, "Sam" Itoh

U

Udelovic, Gertrude
Ullman, David
Ullman, Janet
Ullman, Marian Cohen

V

W

Wagner, Robert
Walker, Steve
Waugh, Alex
Weinger, Dara Michele Papel
Weinger, Todd
Weinstock, Rosa Roth
Weinstock, Susanna *(p)*
Weinstock, Willie
Wilheight, Sam *(p)*
Williams, Boby
Winkler, Rudy *(p)*
Wulf, Sven

Y

Young, Barney

Z

Acknowledgments

Over the past 25 years many people have participated in working with me on this book:

Geoffrey Bellah—Cousin by marriage on the Papel side and retired English professor who edited and corrected the manuscript.

Fiona Stokes Gilbert—Product Development Manager and artist at Papel Giftware who I have worked with for over 40 years and who helped coordinate the design of ancestry charts, the website, and other improvements.

Cheryl Socher Harwood—Cousin who provided supporting information on the Papel side of the family.

Geri Roth Jacobson—Cousin who provided supporting information on the Roth and Fisch sides of the family.

Ron Lapid—Cousin and family historian on the Papel side who provided supporting information and ancestry charts.

Patricia Marshall at Luminare Press—who with her staff helped to bring the manuscript, photographs, and ancestry charts together for publication.

Dave Mason—Author of *Little Shop on Main Street,* the story of Ruggles China and Gifts in Disneyland, portions of which are referenced in the chapters on the lives of Phil and Stan Papel.

Phil Papel—Father whose 60-plus years in "The Life of Phil Papel" was written by him. (My mother and I worked together to complete the rest of his life story.)

Sophie Papel—Mother who is still living and remembering at age 101. For the countless information provided on the lives of my grandparents, my dad, herself, and me. Author of her life story covering her first 15 years and of the life story of Michael Roth.

Rick Scott—A good friend who coordinated *Tales Beyond Main Street,* portions of which are contained in the "Career Years," and who provided assistance in ancestry research and in verifying information.

Sven Wulf—My husband who has patiently put up with me during the many times I have been obsessed with completing this book. For his skill in technology in coordinating the download of photographs, and in organizing the book's format to prepare it for publication.

About the Author

Stanley Louis Papel was born on December 17, 1942 in Los Angeles, California.

He spent his career of over 50 years in the giftware industry creating unique designs with a large national and international distribution. Since retiring, Stanley has been writing about his family history and the family business. His first book, *Tales Beyond Main Street*, is the history of the family business that started in Disneyland in 1955. *Generation to Generation* recounts the story of his ancestors from their European roots to the present.

Stanley is the father of three grown children and several grandchildren. He recently married his husband Sven in 2018. They spend the majority of their time between their homes in Palm Springs and Los Angeles.

A second edition of *Generation to Generation* is in the planning which will include the Papel family in South Africa and Israel.

Visit the websites below to contact the author, see additional photos, ancestry charts, and updates on this book and others to come.

Contact Information

Further contact info available at each website below:

www.GenerationToGeneration.online

www.stanleypapel.com

Made in the USA
Columbia, SC
24 November 2020